ALL THUMBS

Guide to
Repairing Major
Home Appliances

Other All Thumbs Guides
Home Wiring
Home Plumbing
Painting, Wallpapering and Stenciling

ALL THUMBS

Guide to
Repairing Major
Home Appliances

Robert W. Wood

Illustrations by Steve Hoeft

TAB Books
Division of McGraw-Hill, Inc.
Blue Ridge Summit, PA 17294-0850

pbk 4 5 6 7 8 9 10 11 12 DOC/DOC 9 9 8 7 6 5

Library of Congress Cataloging-in-Publication Data

Wood, Robert W., 1933-
   Repairing major home appliances / by Robert W. Wood.
         p.   cm.
   Includes index.
   ISBN 0-8306-2550-X   ISBN 0-8306-2549-6 (pbk.)
   1. Electric apparatus and appliances—Amateurs' manuals.
2. Household appliances—Maintenance and repair—Amateurs' manuals.
I. Title.
TK9901.W657   1992   92-285
643'.6—dc20   CIP

Acquisitions Editor: Kimberly Tabor
Designer: Jaclyn J. Boone
Editorial Team: Susan D. Wahlman, Editor
                 Joanne Slike
Production Team: Katherine G. Brown, Director
                  Janice Ridenour, Layout
                  Jana L. Fisher, Typesetting
Cover Design: Lori E. Schlosser
Cover Illustration: Denny Bond, East Petersburg, Pa.   ATS
Cartoon Caricature: Michael Malle, Pittsburgh, Pa.   4061

The All Thumbs Guarantee

TAB Books/McGraw-Hill guarantees that you will be able to follow every step of each project in this book, from beginning to end, or you will receive your money back. If you are unable to follow the All Thumbs steps, return this book, your store receipt, and a brief explanation to:

All Thumbs
P.O. Box 581
Blue Ridge Summit, PA 17214-9998

About the Binding

This and every All Thumbs book has a special lay-flat binding. To take full advantage of this binding, open the book to any page and run your finger along the spine, pressing down as you do so; the book will stay open at the page you've selected.

The lay-flat binding is designed to withstand constant use. Unlike regular book bindings, the spine will not weaken or crack when you press down on the spine to keep the book open.

Contents

Preface *ix*

Introduction *xi*

1 Electric Water Heaters *1*

2 Clothes Washers *19*

3 Clothes Dryers *39*

4 Refrigerators *59*

5 Ice Makers *78*

6 Dishwashers *86*

7 Electric Ranges *105*

Glossary *123*

Index *127*

Preface

A collection of books about do-it-yourself home repair and improvement, the All Thumbs series was created not for the skilled jack-of-all-trades, but for the average homeowner. If your familiarity with the various systems in the home is minimal, or your budget doesn't keep pace with today's climbing costs, this series is tailor-made for you.

Several different types of professional contractors are required to construct even the smallest home. Carpenters build the framework, plumbers install the pipes, and electricians complete the wiring. Few people can do it all. The necessary skills often require years to master. The professional works quickly and efficiently and depends on a large volume of work to survive. Because service calls are time-consuming, often requiring more travel time than actual labor, they can be expensive. The All Thumbs series saves you time and money by showing you how to make most common repairs yourself.

The guides cover topics such as home wiring; plumbing; painting, stenciling, and wallpapering; and repairing major appliances, to name a few. Copiously illustrated, each book details the procedures in an easy-to-follow, step-by-step format, making many repairs and home improvements well within the ability of nearly any homeowner.

Introduction

Designed for the average homeowner, this book addresses the
need for practical information on the inner workings and
repairs of major electrical home appliances. To make effective
diagnoses and avoid time-consuming guesswork, you must first
understand the construction and operation of the appliance. Since a
number of manufacturers market the same appliance, an attempt
to cover them all would require a large volume indeed. However, all
appliances operate on the same principle. With common sense and a
basic understanding of how the appliance works, most repairs are not
difficult at all.

Try to get a mental picture of what the appliance was designed to
do. Was it designed to heat or cool, run a motor, or both? Normally
that's all appliances do. If it is supposed to heat or cool, is it receiving
electricity? If it is receiving electricity, does it have a thermostat?
If it has a motor, does the motor run or make a noise? By checking
probable causes in a logical order, you should be able to find most
problems in a few minutes.

Before making repairs, you will need to perform a number of
tests with a volt-ohmmeter, so you should familiarize yourself with
the owner's manual that comes with the meter. The main points to
remember: When making voltage tests, always keep your fingers on

the insulated part of the probes; and be sure the meter is on the proper voltage scale, not on the resistance scale. When measuring resistance, or continuity, turn the knob to the resistance scale. Then zero the meter by touching the probes together and adjusting the meter to 0 before making the test.

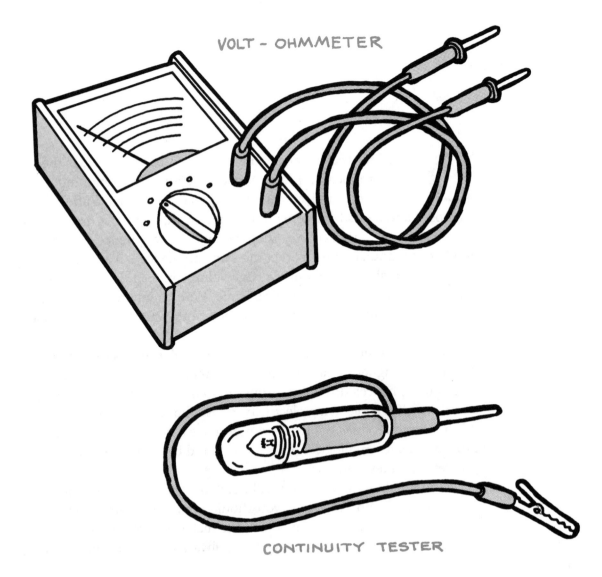

VOLT - OHMMETER

CONTINUITY TESTER

To use a continuity tester, first make sure that no voltage is present. The appliance should be turned off and unplugged. Then touch the probes together to see if the tester's bulb lights. If the bulb lights, the tester is working properly. Next, connect the probe to each terminal on the switch (or whatever you are testing) to see if the bulb lights again. A lit bulb indicates continuity.

Most of the parts that you'll need can be purchased at your local appliance parts supply store. Just look in your phone directory under Appliance-Major-Parts. You'll need to know the make and model of the appliance and the number of the part, if it has one. If the store doesn't stock the particular part you need, someone there should be able to order it for you.

Before making any repairs, consult the owner's manual that came with the appliance. It usually offers troubleshooting tips. Also check to see if the appliance is still under warranty. In most cases, any repairs made by an unauthorized service will void the warranty.

At times, professional help is necessary, but even then, you need a better understanding of your appliance. You will be able to help pinpoint the problem and are less likely to be overcharged by an unscrupulous repair shop.

The book begins with electric water heaters, then covers laundry appliances, and ends with kitchen appliances. Each chapter includes a tools list and illustrated step-by-step instructions explaining how to repair the most common problems that occur with each particular appliance. The troubleshooting guides near the beginning of each chapter will help you determine what you need to look for on the malfunctioning appliance.

CHAPTER ONE

Electric Water Heaters

Electric water heaters normally have two heating elements, with each element controlled by a thermostat. Mounted on the outer wall of the tank above each element, the thermostats sense the water temperature through the wall of the tank. To reduce energy demands, the thermostats work in tandem, one thermostat operating at a time. First the upper thermostat turns on the top element to heat the water in the top of the tank. When the water gets hot, the thermostat turns off the top element, and the bottom element comes on to heat the remaining cold water at the bottom of the tank.

The hot water leaves from the top of the tank and cold water enters from a tube near the bottom of the tank. The bottom thermostat senses the cold water and turns on the element. If enough hot water is used so that the water at the top drops below the setting of the upper thermostat, the top element comes back on to provide additional heat. As a safety measure, a high-temperature cutoff on the upper thermostat turns off the power to the water heater when the water temperature reaches 210 degrees Fahrenheit.

Before you begin any repairs, always turn off the power to the heater at the circuit breaker. Don't remove any access panels until the power is off.

Tools & Materials

- ☐ Volt-ohmmeter
- ☐ Screwdriver
- ☐ Bucket or garden hose
- ☐ Adjustable wrench
- ☐ Pipe wrench
- ☐ Pipe tape

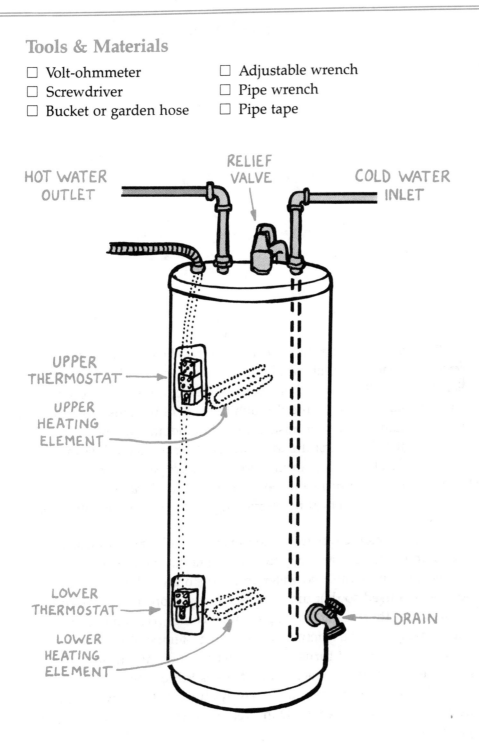

HOT WATER OUTLET

RELIEF VALVE

COLD WATER INLET

UPPER THERMOSTAT

UPPER HEATING ELEMENT

LOWER THERMOSTAT

LOWER HEATING ELEMENT

DRAIN

TROUBLESHOOTING GUIDE

Problem	Probable causes	Solutions
No hot water	Tripped circuit breaker or blown fuse	Reset breaker or replace blown fuse. If it fails again, call an electrician.
	High-temperature cutoff on	Push reset button on high-temperature cutoff. If button trips again, check thermostats and elements.
	High-temperature cutoff faulty	Check high-temperature cutoff.
	Thermostat not turning on element	Check thermostats; replace if necessary.
	Heating element faulty	Check elements; replace if necessary.
Not enough hot water	Low thermostat setting	Adjust thermostat.
	Heating element bad	Check elements for continuity.
	Water heater too small	Replace water heater with larger one or stagger use.
Not enough hot water and noisy plumbing	Scale on elements	Soak elements in vinegar and scrub off scale.
	Scale inside tank; sediment in tank	Drain tank until water runs clear.
Water too hot	Thermostat set too high	Adjust thermostat.
	Thermostat failed	Check thermostat; replace if necessary.
	Insulation missing from around thermostats	Pack insulation tight around thermostats.
Water leaks	Heating element gasket leaking	Replace element gasket.
	Drain valve leaking	Tighten or replace drain valve.
	Relief valve opening	Check or replace relief valve.

Step 1-1. Getting started.

First turn off the circuit breaker to the water heater. Remove both access panels to the thermostats. Push the insulation back clear of the thermostats. Fiberglass can irritate the skin, so wear gloves for protection.

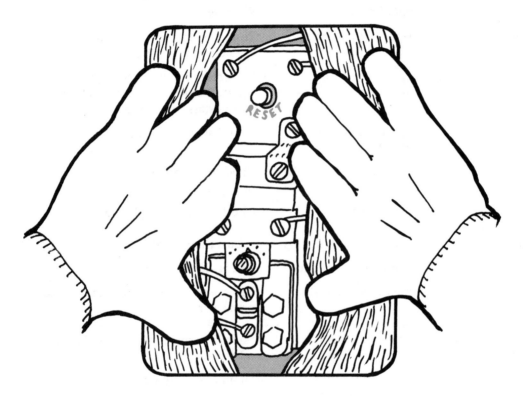

Step 1-2. Checking for power.

Set the volt-ohmmeter on 250 volts ac. Hold the meter probes by the insulated covers and touch a probe to each of the top two terminal screws of the high-temperature cutoff. These screws are where the two wires from the electrical panel are connected. Now touch one probe to the exposed metal wall of the tank (or a mounting bolt) and the other probe to each of the terminals. In all cases, the meter should read 0 volts. (If it doesn't, don't touch anything—the power is still on.) If voltage is not present, turn the power back on and carefully repeat the test. The meter should read 220 volts across the terminals and 120 volts between each terminal and the wall of the tank. If it doesn't, you'll probably need an electrician, because power is not getting to the water heater. If voltage is present, go to the next step. Remember, do all work with the power off.

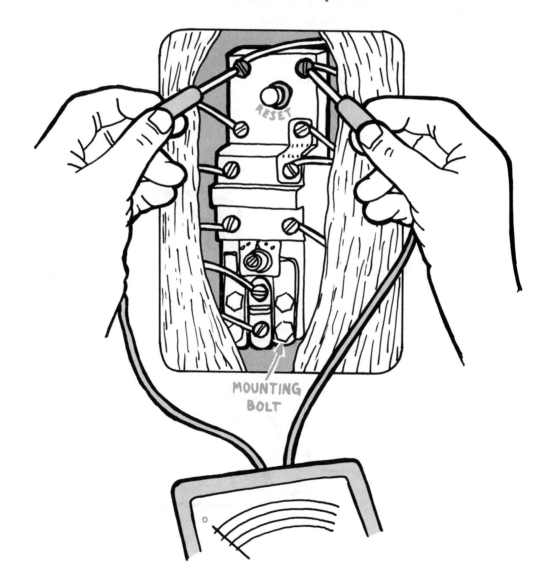

MOUNTING
BOLT

Step 1-3. Checking the reset button.

Turn off the breaker at the service panel. Retest for voltage at the water heater to make sure none is present. Then push in the cutoff reset button. If you hear it click, water might have seeped into one of the heating elements, causing a short. The short will show up later, when you check the elements.

Step 1-4. Checking the high-temperature cutoff.

Disconnect one of the wires to the heating element (it doesn't matter which one). Set the volt-ohmmeter on the R×1 scale and touch a probe to each of the two screw terminals to the left of the reset button. Repeat the test on the two terminals to the right of the button. The meter needle should move to 0 each time, showing a connection. If it does, your next step is to check the thermostat and elements (Step 1-6). If it doesn't, replace the high-temperature cutoff.

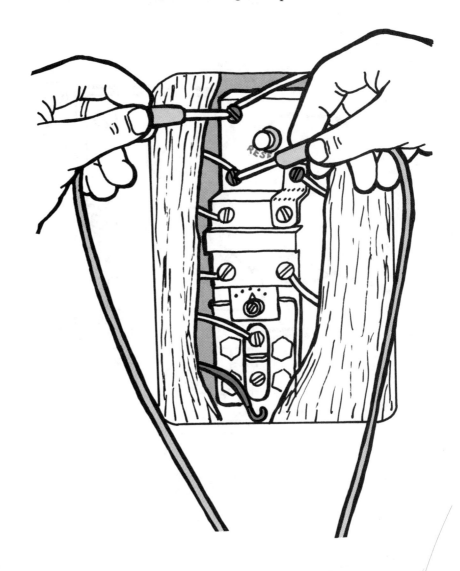

Step 1-5. Replacing the high-temperature cutoff.
Before disconnecting any wires, label the wires and draw a
wiring diagram. Now disconnect the wires and the two metal
straps going to the thermostat. Pull up on the cutoff and remove
it from the spring clips holding it in place. Push in the reset button
on the new cutoff and install it behind the spring clips. Connect the
metal straps and wires to their corresponding places on the new cutoff.

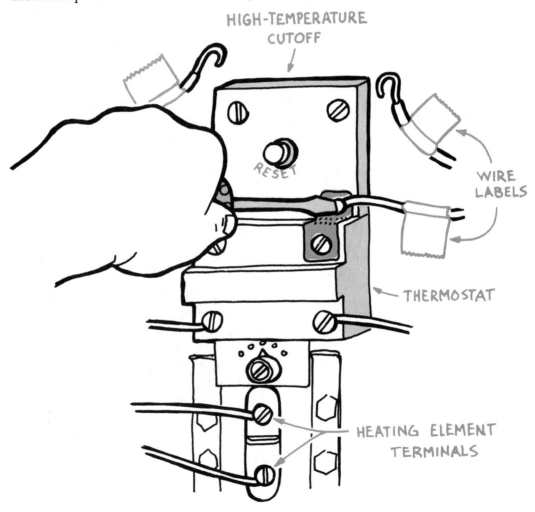

HIGH-TEMPERATURE
CUTOFF

RESET

WIRE
LABELS

THERMOSTAT

HEATING ELEMENT
TERMINALS

Step 1-6. Checking the top thermostat.
Make sure the power to the heater is off.
Disconnect the wire to the top element.
Use a screwdriver to turn the thermostat
clockwise to its highest setting.

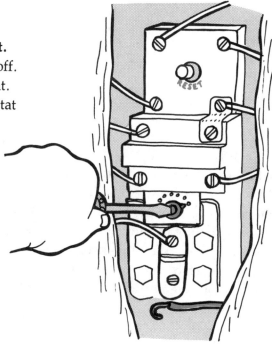

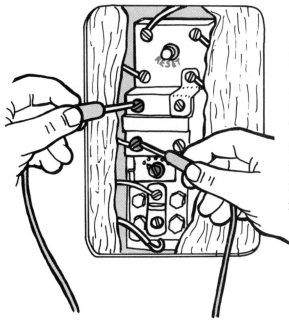

Step 1-7. Completing the test.
With the meter set on R×1, touch one
of the probes to each of the two screw
terminals on the left side of the thermostat.
The meter should move to 0. Now turn the
thermostat to its lowest setting and repeat
the tests. This time, the meter should not
move. If the thermostat fails the tests,
install a new one.

Step 1-8.
Checking the bottom thermostat.

Make sure the power to the heater is off.
Disconnect one of the wires to the bottom element.
Turn both the top and bottom thermostats to their
lowest settings. With the meter set on R×1, touch a
probe to each of the two terminal screws on the bottom
thermostat. The needle on the meter should not move.

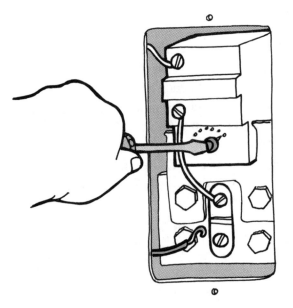

Step 1-9.
Completing the test.

Now turn the bottom thermostat to its
highest setting. The needle should move
to 0. If not, replace the bottom thermostat
with a new one. If the thermostats are
good, check the elements (Step 1-12).

Step 1-10. Removing the thermostat.

Make sure the power is off. Before disconnecting any wires, label the wires and draw a wiring diagram. To remove the top thermostat, first remove the screws connecting the two metal straps to the high-temperature cutoff and the two wires from the thermostat. Slide the high-temperature cutoff up out of the way. (The bottom thermostat, shown here, does not have a high-temperature cutoff.) Loosen the two bolts on the thermostat's bracket. The bracket holds the thermostat against the wall of the tank. Now slide the thermostat up and out from behind the bracket.

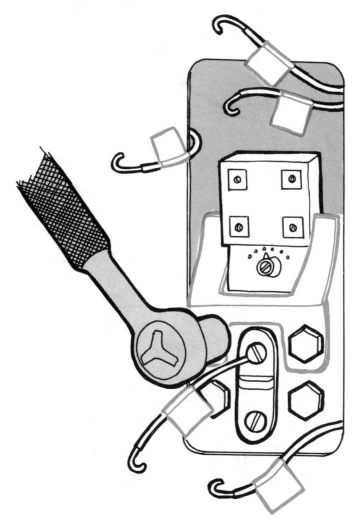

Step 1-11. Installing a thermostat.
Making sure that the back of the thermostat is flush against
the wall of the heater, tighten the mounting bolts on the bracket,
and press the cutoff back into place. Reconnect the wires and
set both thermostats to about 140 degrees.

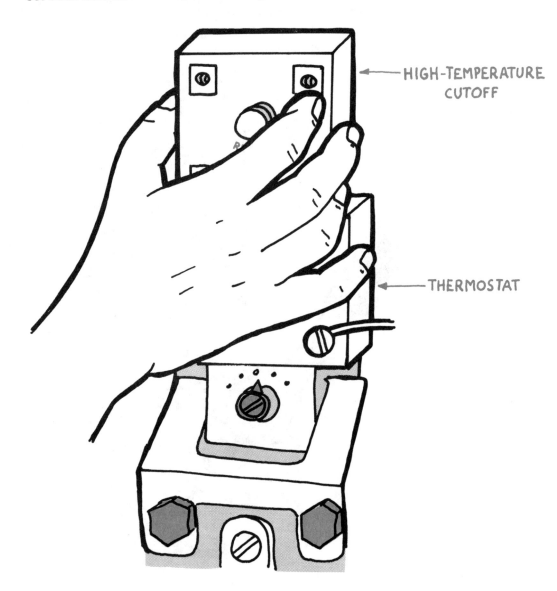

HIGH-TEMPERATURE CUTOFF

THERMOSTAT

Step 1-12. Checking heating elements.

To check for continuity, make sure the power to the heater is off
at the service panel. Remove both access panels on the heater.
Check again for voltage. Wearing gloves, carefully pull the insulation
back to get to the terminals. Disconnect one of the wires to each
element. Set the meter to R×1 and touch a probe to each of the
two screw terminals on the elements. The needle should move to
somewhere in the middle of the scale—about 10 to 20 ohms. If it
doesn't, replace the element with a new one. If the element tests
as good, check it for a short.

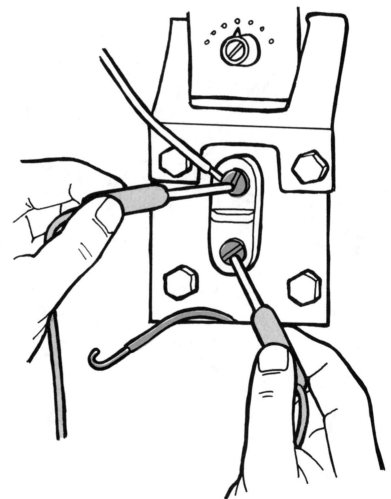

Step 1-13. Checking the element for a short.
While the power to the heater is still off, adjust the meter to a higher setting (R×1K or more) and touch one probe to one of the element's mounting bolts and the other probe to one of the element's terminals. The needle should not move at all. If it does, a short circuit exists between the element and the tank. Install a new element.

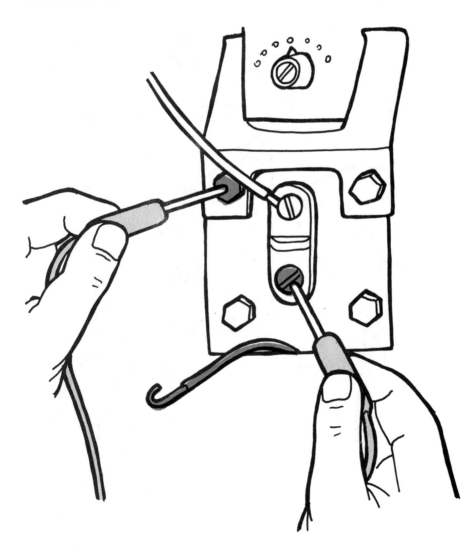

GASKET

ELEMENT

Step 1-14.
Draining the tank.
Make sure the power to the heater is off.
Shut off the cold water supply to the heater at the
valve on the cold water pipe coming into the heater.
Open a hot water faucet at a convenient sink to equalize
the air pressure in the system. Attach a garden hose to
the heater's drain or place a bucket underneath the drain.
Open the drain. If the water drains slowly, open more faucets.
If you are draining the heater with a bucket, watch to make sure
that the bucket doesn't overflow. After the tank has drained,
disconnect the two wires from the element. Remove the four
bolts holding the element and the thermostat bracket.
Now remove the element and the old gasket.

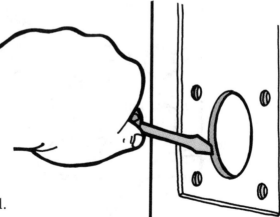

Step 1-15.
Ensuring a tight seal.
Scrape away any scale or rust around
the opening with an old screwdriver so
that the new gasket will make a tight seal.

Step 1-16. Installing a new element.

Install the new element and gasket. Mount the thermostat bracket and thermostat. Connect the two wires to the element. Push the insulation back in place and install the access panels. Close the drain on the tank and open the water supply to refill the tank. When water runs from the hot water faucet at the sink, the tank is full. If you turned on additional faucets to make the tank drain faster, be sure to turn them back off. Turn the power back on.

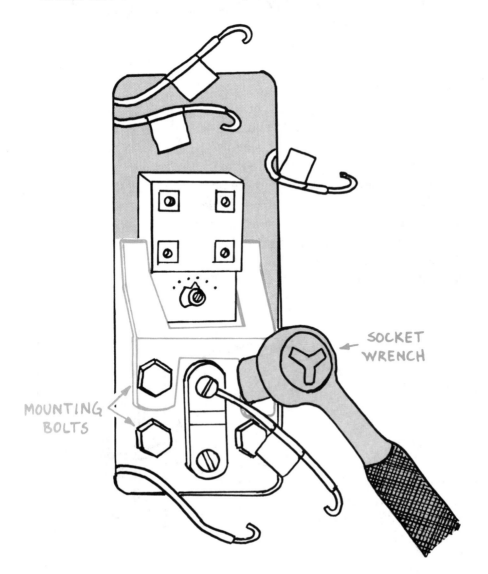

SOCKET WRENCH

MOUNTING BOLTS

Step 1-17. Testing the pressure relief valve.
Stand clear of the valve outlet. Remember that the water is hot.
Now lift the spring lever. About a cup of hot water should spurt out.
Operate the lever a few times to remove any sediment in the valve.
If the water does not come out or the valve drips, replace it.
NOTE: If the heater is old, the valve might stick open. If it does,
quickly shut off the cold water supply and go to the next step.

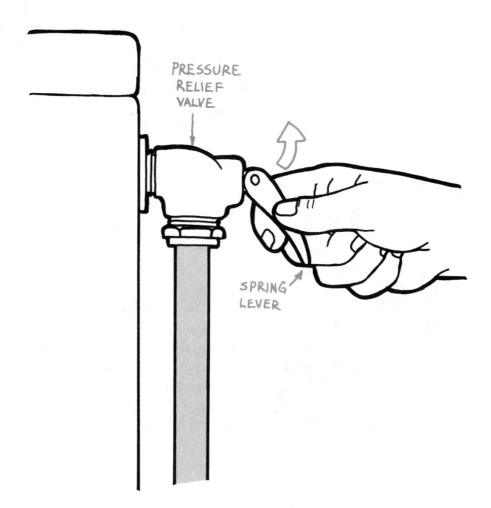

PRESSURE
RELIEF
VALVE

SPRING
LEVER

Step 1-18. Removing the old valve.

First turn off the power and close the cold water valve to the tank. Drain a gallon or so of water from the tank if the relief valve is on the top of the water heater. Drain about five gallons if the relief valve is on the side of the tank. Use an adjustable wrench to remove the discharge pipe. Use a pipe wrench to turn the relief valve counterclockwise. Apply firm, steady pressure to loosen the valve. Remove the valve and take it with you when you buy a new one.

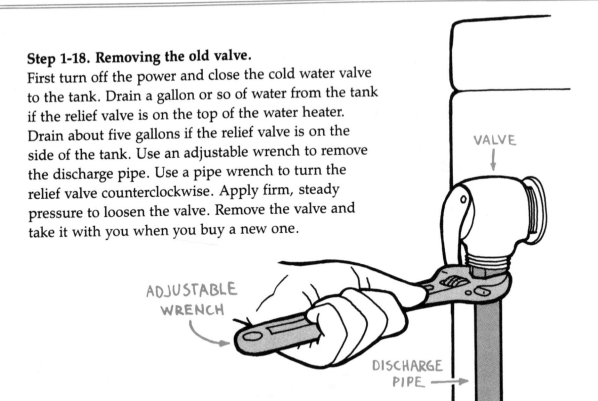

VALVE

ADJUSTABLE WRENCH

DISCHARGE PIPE

Step 1-19. Installing the new valve.

Wrap a couple of turns of pipe tape clockwise over the threads of the new valve. Thread the new valve into the opening in the tank. Use a pipe wrench to tighten the valve. Reinstall the discharge pipe and open the cold water valve. Turn the power back on.

CHAPTER TWO

Clothes Washers

When you turn on a washer, you start a timer connected to switches that control the operation of the machine. First, a water mixing valve opens, letting a mixture of hot and cold water into the tub. When the water reaches the preset level, the switch closes the mixing valve. The timer then turns on a motor that operates an agitator, which churns the clothes back and forth in the basket. At the end of the wash cycle, the timer turns on the pump to drain the tub. The basket spins at high speed, removing any excess water by centrifugal force. The pump pushes the water from the machine into a standpipe connected to a house drain. A safety switch stops the machine if the lid is raised.

Three systems operate together in a clothes washer. The electrical system, controlled by the timer and switches, operates the motor and valves; the mechanical system, which includes the transmission and drive belt, operates the agitator and the basket; and the plumbing system moves the water through the pump and hoses. The most common problems with clothes washers are leaks in the hoses and pump (the plumbing system), followed by a slipping or broken drive belt (the mechanical system), then a faulty timer (the electrical system). An important guide to the electrical system is the wiring diagram provided by the manufacturer. You usually can find the diagram inside the control panel, but it might be attached to the inside of the back panel.

Most repairs can be made by the homeowner, unless the transmission is involved. Please note that no repairs should be attempted while the machine is running, particularly if water is on the floor.

Tools & Materials

- ☐ Screwdriver
- ☐ Pliers
- ☐ Needle-nose pliers
- ☐ Socket wrench and sockets
- ☐ Volt-ohmmeter

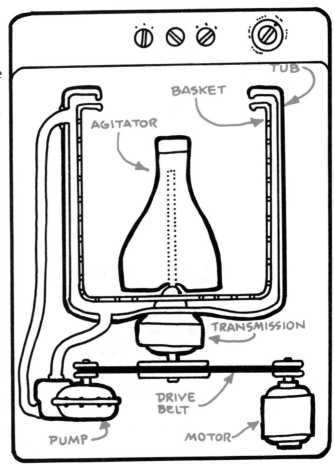

TROUBLESHOOTING GUIDE

Problem	Probable causes	Solutions
Washer doesn't run	No power to washer	Make sure washer is plugged in and circuit breaker has not tripped.
	Lid switch activated	Make sure lid is closed. Check lid switch.
	Timer faulty	Check timer and timer motor.
	Motor faulty	Check motor; replace if necessary.

TROUBLESHOOTING GUIDE CONTINUED.

Washer doesn't fill	Water turned off	Turn on faucet.
	Hoses kinked	Remove any kinks in hose.
	Screens or water inlet valve clogged	Clean screens or water inlet valve.
	Water inlet valve faulty	Check water inlet valve.
	Timer faulty	Rotate the timer dial slightly and press control button in firmly. Check timer.
	Water temperature switch faulty	Check water temperature switch.
	Water level switch, hose, or pressure dome faulty	Check water level switch and hose assembly.
Washer doesn't agitate	Slipping or broken drive belt	Tighten or replace drive belt.
	Timer faulty	Check timer.
	Lid switch faulty	Check lid switch.
	Motor or transmission faulty	Check motor. If transmission faulty call for service.
Water doesn't drain out	Kinked drain hose	Straighten hose.
	Suds blocking drain	Turn off machine, bail out excess suds and water, and flush tub with cold water.
	Timer faulty	Check timer.
	Pump faulty	Replace pump.
Washer leaks	Loose or cracked hose	Tighten or replace hoses.
	Pump leaking	Replace pump.
Washer vibrates excessively	Load unbalanced	Redistribute clothes.
	Washer not level	Adjust washer's leveling feet.
Washer doesn't spin	Loose or broken drive belt	Tighten or replace drive belt.
	Motor or transmission faulty	Replace motor or, if transmission faulty, call for service.

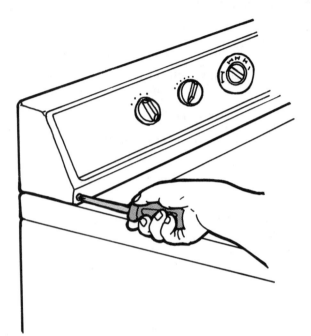

Step 2-1.
Removing the control panel.
Unplug the washer and pull it away from the wall slightly. Remove the control panel by removing the two screws from the bottom front corners of the panel.

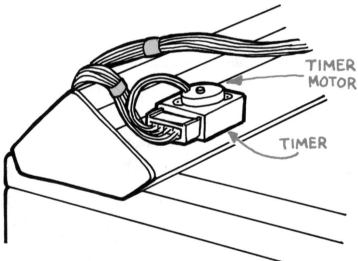

TIMER MOTOR

TIMER

Step 2-2.
Gaining access to the controls.
Remove any other screws on the top or the back of the panel. Pad the top of the washer with an old towel.
Tilt the panel forward and lay it face down on the towel. You now have access to the timer, the timer motor, the water level switch, and the water temperature switches. You also should notice the wiring diagram.

Step 2-3. Testing and replacing the timer.

Locate the terminals on the timer that operate the cycle you want to test. (Refer to wiring diagram.) Disconnect the wiring plug to get to the terminals. Turn the timer control knob clockwise to the cycle you want to test. Set the volt-ohmmeter to R×1 and touch a probe to each of the two terminals for that cycle. The meter should go to 0; if it doesn't, replace the timer with a new one. If it does, test the timer motor.

WIRING
PLUG

To install the new timer, remove the control knob and the screws holding the timer in place. Install the new timer; reconnect the wires and control knob. Reinstall the control panel and plug in the washer.

Step 2-4. Testing the timer motor.
Disconnect the two wires coming from the motor.
Set the volt-ohmmeter to R×100; touch a probe
to each of the two motor wires. The meter needle
should move to about 3000 ohms. If it doesn't,
install a new timer motor. Depending on the
model, you might be able to replace the timer
motor separately. Otherwise, you will have to
replace the complete timer unit (Step 2-3).

WIRE LABEL

Step 2-5.
Testing the water temperature switch.
Unplug the washer and remove the control panel.
Locate the back of the water temperature switch and
determine which terminals control the temperature you want to
test. (Refer to the wiring diagram.) Draw a simple wiring diagram
and label each wire. Disconnect the wires. Turn the temperature
switch to the temperature setting you want to test. Set the volt-
ohmmeter to the R×1 scale and touch a probe to each of the two
terminals. The meter needle should move to 0. If it doesn't, you
need to replace the switch. Remove the old switch. Install the new
switch, making the connections according to your wiring diagram.

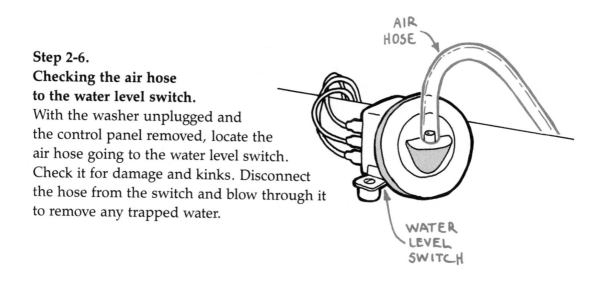

Step 2-6.
Checking the air hose
to the water level switch.
With the washer unplugged and
the control panel removed, locate the
air hose going to the water level switch.
Check it for damage and kinks. Disconnect
the hose from the switch and blow through it
to remove any trapped water.

AIR
HOSE

WATER
LEVEL
SWITCH

Step 2-7. Testing the water level switch.
You should see three wires connected to the back of the
water level switch. Label and disconnect these wires from
the switch. Set the volt-ohmmeter to the R×1 scale or use
a continuity tester. Touch a probe to one terminal and the
other probe to the other two terminals. Test each terminal
to the other two for continuity. You should perform three
tests to cover each possible connection. Two of the tests
should show no connection; on one test the needle should
move to 0, showing continuity. If the needle does not move,
replace the water level switch (Step 2-9).

Step 2-8.
Performing a second test on the water level switch.
If the switch passed the first test, connect a small length of plastic
tubing to the fitting on the switch where the air hose was connected.
Blow very lightly into the tube. If plastic tubing
is not available, blow directly into the fitting
on the switch. The switch should click.
Repeat the continuity test between the
three terminals. This time, two different
terminals should show continuity. If not,
replace the switch with a new one.

Step 2-9. Installing a new water level switch.
Make sure the three wires are labeled. Disconnect them from
the switch. Remove the control knob from the front of the
control panel. Remove the switch from the back of the panel.
Mount the new switch. You might see a calibration screw
on the back of the switch. Don't turn it.
Any adjustment to this screw could
cause the tub to overfill. Reconnect
the wires and the air hose to the
switch. Install the control knob
and put the control panel
back into position.

Step 2-10. Checking the pressure dome.

Raise the top panel of the washer. It is held in place by spring clips near each corner. Wrap a few turns of masking tape around a putty knife and slide it under the top panel in each corner. Push the spring clips back and release the top. You should now have access to the pressure dome, the inlet valve, the lid switch, and the agitator. Look on the right side of the tub and find the air hose from the water level switch. The hose will be connected to the air pressure dome. Check for any cracked or broken seals around the dome. The assembly should be completely airtight. If you see any cracks or breaks, replace the dome. To replace the dome, simply disconnect the hose, push down on the dome and turn it about a quarter turn counterclockwise. Install the new dome by pushing down and turning it a quarter turn clockwise. Reconnect the hose.

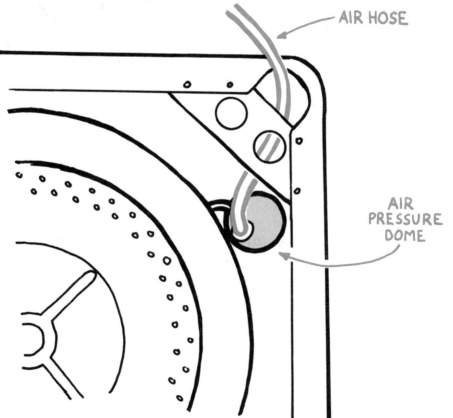

AIR HOSE

AIR
PRESSURE
DOME

Step 2-11. Finding the lid safety switch.

Unplug the washer and open the lid. Depending on the type of washer, you might find two screws on the right side of the lid opening. Loosen these two screws and raise the top panel of the washer. You should see the lid safety switch on the underside of the panel.

LIFT LID

Step 2-12.
Checking the lid safety switch.

Remove the plastic shield and check the switch for damage or loose wires. Disconnect the two wires to the switch.

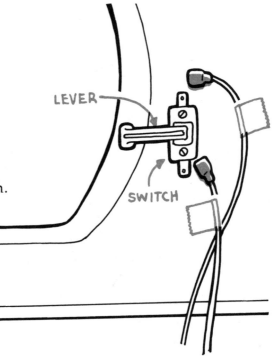

LEVER

SWITCH

Step 2-13. Testing the lid safety switch.

Use a volt-ohmmeter set on R×1 scale or a continuity tester
to test the switch. Touch the probes to each of the two terminals
of the switch. Operate the lid safety switch by hand and monitor
the movement of the meter needle. The needle should show
continuity (move to 0) when the switch is depressed, the position
it would be in with the lid closed. The needle should show no
continuity when the switch is released, the position it would be
in with the lid open. If the switch fails this test, replace it. To
replace the switch, remove it from the washer panel. Install the
new switch, reconnect the wires, and replace the plastic shield.

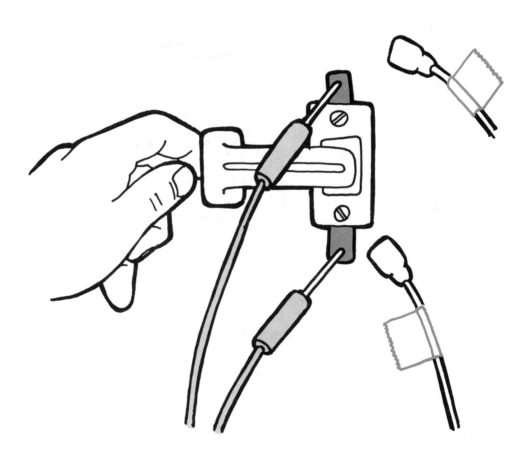

Step 2-14. Checking the water inlet valve.

Unplug the washer and move it out from the wall slightly. Turn off both faucets and disconnect the hoses from the water inlet valve on the back of the washer. Pry out the domed strainers with a small screwdriver or knife. Be careful not to damage the screens. Rinse the clogs from the strainers and reinstall them, dome side up, in the valve.

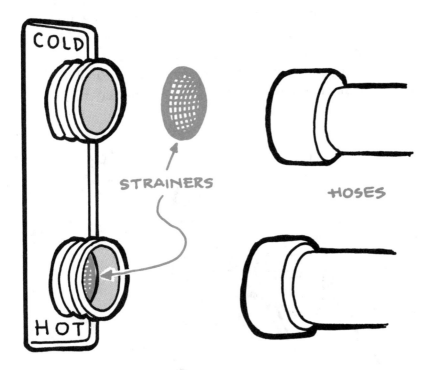

STRAINERS

HOSES

COLD

HOT

Step 2-15. Testing one type of water inlet valve.

Your washer will have an inlet valve in one of two places. With the machine unplugged and the hoses disconnected, remove the back panel from the machine. Now lift the top panel of the machine. Look for the valve on the bottom of a bracket on the left corner of the machine. If it is not there, go to Step 2-16.

If it is there, remove the two screws holding the valve to the bracket. Remove the valve and the attached wires through the back of the machine. Draw a wiring diagram; then disconnect the wires from the valve. Set the volt-ohmmeter to the R×100 scale. The valve should have two solenoids, each with a pair of terminals. Touch the volt-ohmmeter's probes to the two terminals of one solenoid. Then touch the probes to the two terminals of the second solenoid. The needle on the meter should show continuity with some resistance, approximately 800 ohms for each solenoid. If the meter indicates no continuity for either solenoid, install a new valve.

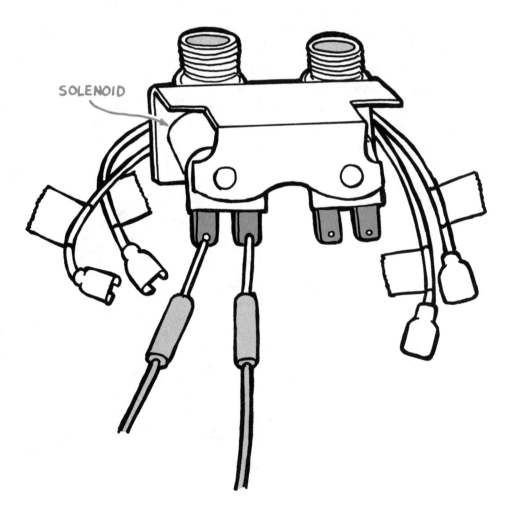

SOLENOID

Step 2-16. Testing another type of water inlet valve.
If you did not find the water inlet valve in Step 2-15, raise the top panel
of the machine and remove the splash guard from the tub rim. The inlet
valve should be located inside the cabinet on the left rear corner of the
machine. Draw a simple wiring diagram and disconnect the wires
from the solenoids. Set the volt-ohmmeter to the R×100 scale and
test the continuity between each pair of terminals (see Step 2-15).
If the meter shows no continuity for either solenoid, replace
the inlet valve with a new one. Disconnect the hoses from
the valve inside the machine, remove the mounting
screws from the back of the machine, and pull
the valve out through the top of the cabinet.
Install the new valve in the reverse order.
Reconnect the wires, making sure they go to
the proper terminals as indicated on your
wiring diagram. Then reconnect the hoses.

WATER
INLET
VALVE

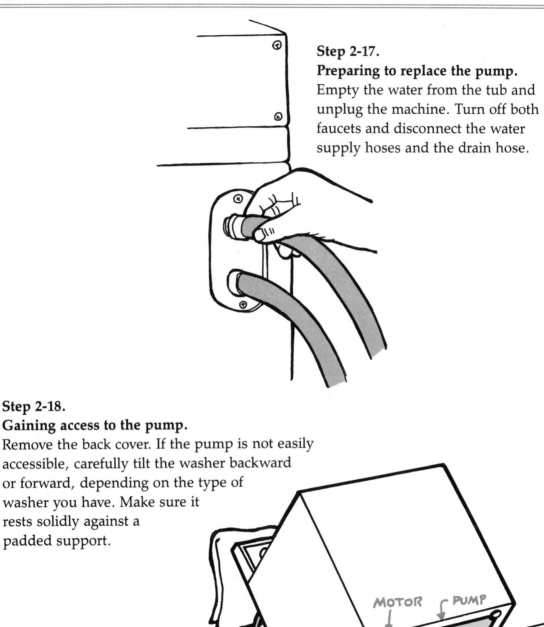

Step 2-17.
Preparing to replace the pump.
Empty the water from the tub and
unplug the machine. Turn off both
faucets and disconnect the water
supply hoses and the drain hose.

Step 2-18.
Gaining access to the pump.
Remove the back cover. If the pump is not easily
accessible, carefully tilt the washer backward
or forward, depending on the type of
washer you have. Make sure it
rests solidly against a
padded support.

MOTOR   PUMP

BLANKET
OR PAD

FILTER

TRANSMISSION

Step 2-19. Disconnecting the hoses from the pump.
Spread a couple of old towels under the pump—some water
will still be trapped in the pump and hoses. Use pliers to
loosen the hose clamps and slide them back on the hoses.
Twist and pull the hoses from the pump.

CLAMP

Step 2-20. Removing the pump.
Loosen the clamp holding the pump coupling to the pump.
Use a socket wrench and socket to loosen the pump mounting bolts.
Support the pump with one hand and remove the mounting bolts.
The pump should drop free.
If the pump was leaking, you
need to install a new one.
Install the new pump by
reconnecting the hoses,
tightening the hose clamps,
mounting the pump,
and fastening the pump
to the coupling.

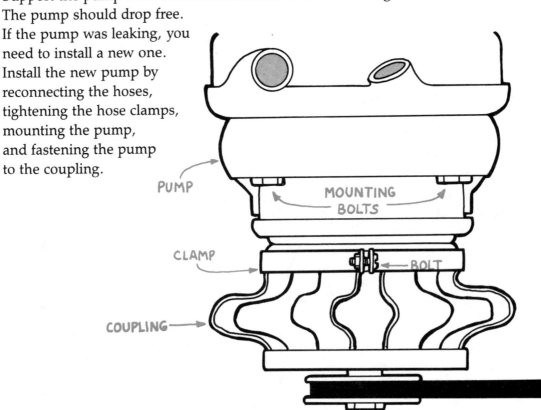

PUMP

MOUNTING
BOLTS

CLAMP

BOLT

COUPLING

Step 2-21. Tightening the drive belt.

Unplug the washer and turn off the faucets. Work the machine away from the wall a few feet and remove the back panel. Press firmly on the drive belt with your thumb. It should not move more than about 1/2 inch. If it does, loosen the motor mount bolts slightly, just enough so that the motor can be shifted. Now shift the motor against the belt to take out the slack. Tighten the motor mounting bolts.

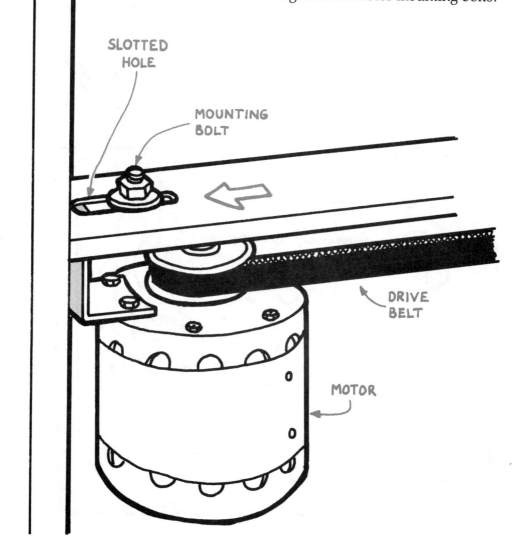

SLOTTED HOLE

MOUNTING BOLT

DRIVE BELT

MOTOR

Step 2-22. Testing the motor for a short.

Unplug the washer. Turn off both faucets and disconnect the hoses. Remove the back panel. You might have to tilt the machine forward to get access to the bottom. Locate the motor. Draw a wiring diagram, then label and disconnect the wires from the motor. To see if the motor is shorted to ground, set the volt-ohmmeter to the R×1K scale. Touch one probe to the metal frame of the motor and touch the other probe to each of the wire terminals. The needle on the meter should not move. If it does move, you need to replace the motor.

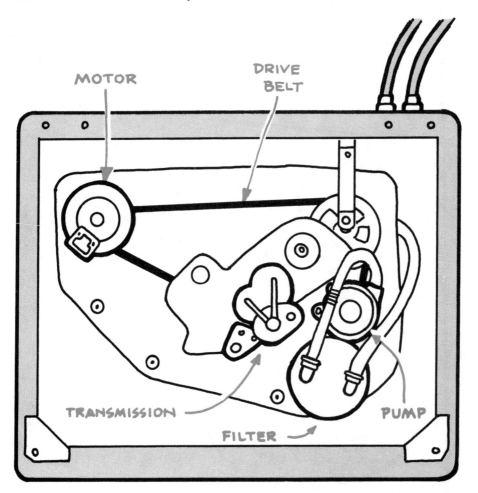

MOTOR

DRIVE BELT

TRANSMISSION

FILTER

PUMP

Step 2-23.

Testing the motor for continuity.

Now set the volt-ohmmeter to the R×1 scale
Among the wires coming from inside the
motor, you should see one white wire.
Hold one of the probes to this wire while
touching the other probe to each of the
other colored wires one at a time. In each
test, the needle on the meter should show
continuity with a low resistance of about
10 or 15 ohms. If continuity is not shown,
replace the motor.

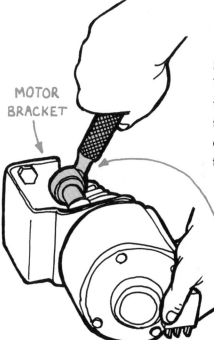

MOTOR
BRACKET

Step 2-24. Removing the old motor.
Working from the opened back of the washer,
use a socket wrench and socket to disconnect
the motor from the motor bracket. Unhook the
drive belt from the motor pulley. Carefully remove
the motor and pulley from the back of the machine.

REMOVE DRIVE BELT
FROM MOTOR PULLEY

Step 2-25. Installing the new motor.

Use a hex wrench to loosen the set screw from the side of the
motor pulley. Remove the pulley. You might need to apply some
penetrating oil and tap lightly with a hammer to free the pulley
from the shaft. Install the pulley on the new motor and tighten the
set screw. If the new motor does not come with a start switch, you
need to remove the one from the old motor and install it on the
new motor. Install the new motor in the reverse order. Follow your
wiring diagram to make sure that all the wires are reconnected to
their proper terminals and that the green ground wire is connected
to the motor housing.

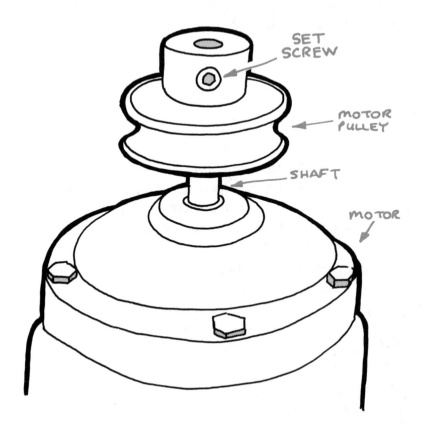

CHAPTER THREE

Clothes Dryers

When you turn on a clothes dryer, you are setting the controls that operate the motor. The motor turns on a blower and rotates the drum. The blower pushes air through the exhaust duct. One or more thermostats linked to a timer control the heating element. As the clothes tumble, hot, dry air enters the drum, circulates through the clothes, and exits through the lint trap and out the exhaust duct.

As always, any time you are working with electricity, make sure the power is off or the appliance is unplugged.

Tools & Materials

- ☐ Towel
- ☐ Screwdriver
- ☐ Putty knife
- ☐ Volt-ohmmeter
- ☐ Continuity tester
- ☐ Adjustable wrench
- ☐ Needle-nose pliers
- ☐ Wire cutters

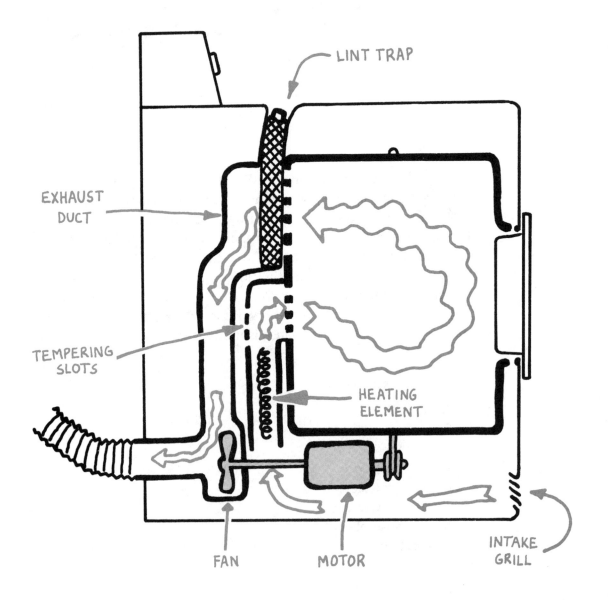

LINT TRAP

EXHAUST
DUCT

TEMPERING
SLOTS

HEATING
ELEMENT

FAN

MOTOR

INTAKE
GRILL

TROUBLESHOOTING GUIDE

Problem	Probable causes	Solutions
Dryer doesn't run	No power to dryer	Make sure dryer is plugged in. Check circuit breakers.
	Door opened or door switch faulty	Close door. Check door switch.
	Timer or timer motor faulty	Test timer and timer motor.
	Dryer motor faulty	Test motor; replace if necessary.
Dryer runs but doesn't heat	Temperature selector switch faulty	Check temperature selector switch.
	Timer faulty	Check timer and timer motor.
	Thermostat faulty	Check thermostat.
	Heating element faulty	Check heating element.
Dryer runs but doesn't dry clothes	Blocked lint trap or exhaust duct	Clean lint from trap and duct.
	Thermostats faulty	Check thermostats.
	Heater element faulty	Check heating element.
Drum doesn't rotate	Broken belt	Replace belt.
	Broken tension spring	Replace spring.
	Dryer motor faulty	Check and replace motor if necessary.

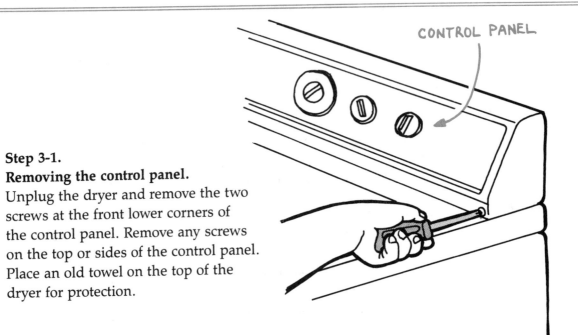

CONTROL PANEL

Step 3-1.
Removing the control panel.
Unplug the dryer and remove the two screws at the front lower corners of the control panel. Remove any screws on the top or sides of the control panel. Place an old towel on the top of the dryer for protection.

Step 3-2. Gaining access to the controls.
Disconnect the control panel from the top of the dryer and place it face down on the towel. Remove the screws holding the rear panel in place. You now have access to the timer, temperature selector switch, and start switch.

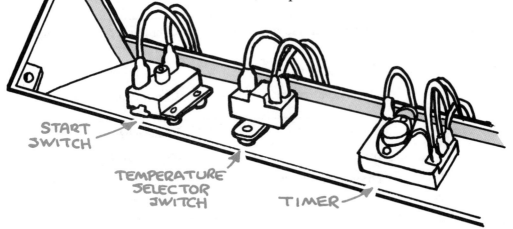

START SWITCH

TEMPERATURE SELECTOR SWITCH

TIMER

Step 3-3. Testing the timer.

Label the wires going to the timer, draw a wiring diagram, then disconnect the wires. Set the volt-ohmmeter to the R×1 scale and turn the timer knob to the first setting. Touch one probe to each terminal on the timer. The needle should indicate continuity (move to 0) between at least one pair of terminals. Turn the control knob to the next setting and repeat the test. You should get continuity between one pair of terminals at each setting except OFF. When the timer is off, no pair of terminals should show continuity. If the timer fails the test, replace it. To replace the timer, remove the control knob from the front of the panel. Disconnect the old timer from the back of the panel. Install the new timer and reconnect the wires according to your wiring diagram.

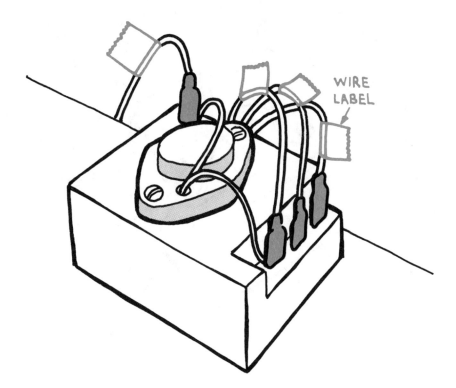

WIRE
LABEL

Step 3-4. Testing the timer motor.

Disconnect the two wires going to the timer motor terminals. Set the volt-ohmmeter to the R×1K scale. Touch a probe to each of the two motor terminals. The needle should move to approximately 2500 ohms. If the needle fails to move, replace the motor. Remove the two screws holding the motor in place, install the new motor, and reconnect the wires. For some models, you might have to replace the entire timer.

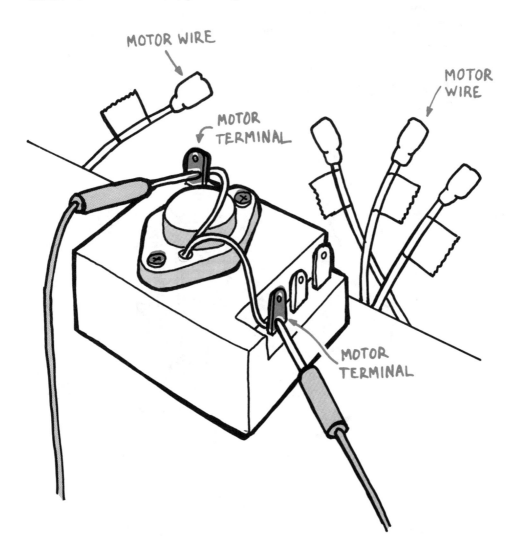

MOTOR WIRE

MOTOR WIRE

MOTOR TERMINAL

MOTOR TERMINAL

Step 3-5. Testing the temperature selector switch.

Label the wires and draw a wiring diagram showing where the wires connect to the switch. Disconnect the wires from the switch terminals. Set the temperature control to the heat setting you want to test. Set the volt-ohmmeter to the R×1 scale. Touch one probe to one terminal and the other probe to the other terminal that corresponds with the temperature selected. (If you have a dial selector, refer to the manufacturer's wiring diagram in the control panel.)

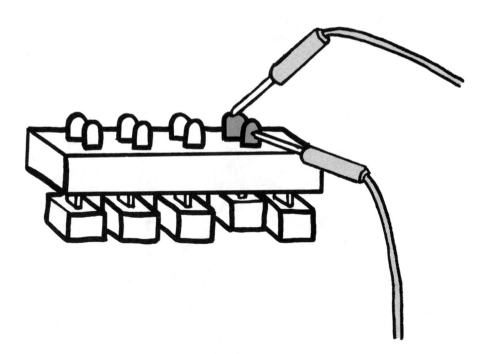

The meter should move to 0, indicating continuity. Repeat this test for each temperature setting on the selector switch. If no continuity exists at any temperature setting, replace the selector switch. Disconnect the old switch from the control panel. Install the new switch and reconnect the wires.

Step 3-6. Checking the start switch.

Label the wires and disconnect them from the switch's terminals. Set the volt-ohmmeter to the R×1 scale. If the switch has two terminals, touch a probe to each terminal. The needle should not move. Now press the start button and repeat the test. The needle now should move to 0. If the switch has three terminals, touch a probe to the terminal marked NC and the other probe to the terminal marked CO. The meter should swing to 0. Now press the start button. The needle should swing in the other direction, indicating no continuity. If your results are different, install a new switch.

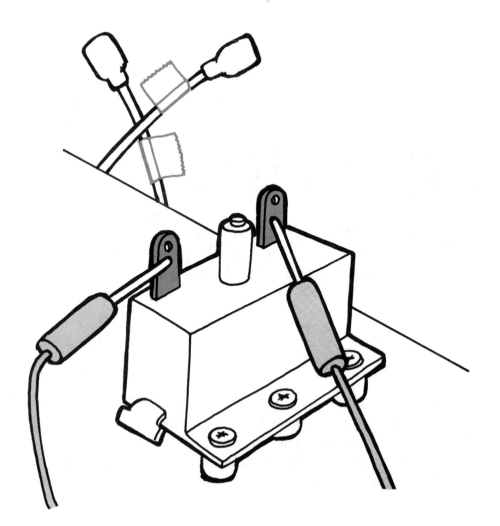

Step 3-7. Gaining access to the door switch.
Unplug the dryer. If your dryer has a top-mounted lint screen,
remove the screen and the screws at the edge of the screen slot.
Wrap a few turns of masking tape around the blade of a putty knife.
Insert the blade under the top panel a couple of inches from each
corner and push in on the hidden clips to release the top panel.

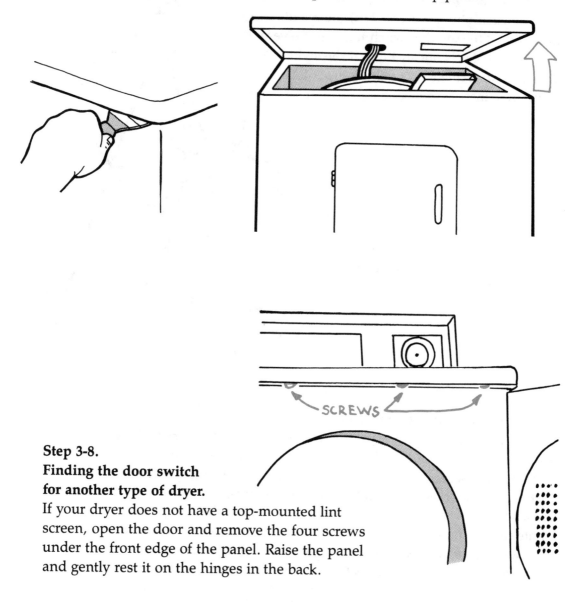

Step 3-8.
Finding the door switch
for another type of dryer.
If your dryer does not have a top-mounted lint
screen, open the door and remove the four screws
under the front edge of the panel. Raise the panel
and gently rest it on the hinges in the back.

Step 3-9. Testing the door switch.

The switch should be mounted near the upper corner
of the door opening. Disconnect the two wires from the
switch terminals. Using a continuity tester or a volt-ohmmeter
set to the R×1 scale, touch a probe to each terminal of
the switch. With the door open, the needle should not
move, indicating no continuity. With the door closed,
or the switch plunger pressed in, the needle should
move to 0. Operate the switch manually several times
to ensure that it is not sticking. If the switch
does not work freely or it fails to check for
continuity, install a new one.

CONTINUITY
TESTER

FRONT
PANEL

SWITCH

DISCONNECTED
LEADS

Step 3-10. Testing the thermostats.

Depending on the type of dryer, the thermostats might be located on
the blower housing and the heater box, on the heater housing, or
under the lint screen. Unplug the dryer and disconnect the exhaust
duct. Move the dryer out from the wall to gain access to the rear panel.
Use a small socket wrench or screwdriver to remove the rear panel.
Locate the thermostats. You might find three or four—test them all the
same way. You should see two wires going to each thermostat. Select a
thermostat to test and disconnect one of the wires from its terminal.

Set the volt-ohmmeter to the R×1 scale, or use a continuity tester. Touch one probe to each terminal of the thermostat. If you are using a volt-ohmmeter, the needle should move to 0, indicating continuity. If you are using a continuity tester, the bulb should light. If any thermostat fails the test, remove it and install a new one.

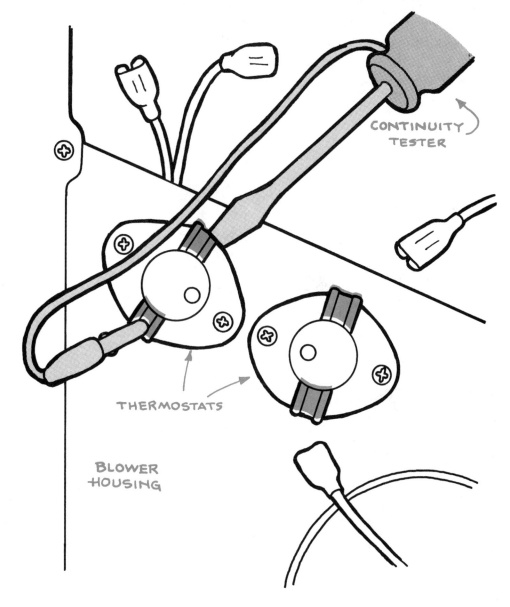

CONTINUITY TESTER

THERMOSTATS

BLOWER HOUSING

Step 3-11. Testing the heating element.

With the dryer unplugged and rear panel removed, locate the heater box and the wires going to the heater terminals. If you don't see a heater box, the dryer has heating coils located in a heater housing behind the drum. If the dryer has heating coils, go to Step 3-14.

If you see a heater box, label and disconnect the wires to the heating element's terminals. Set the volt-ohmmeter to the R×1 scale. If the element has two terminals, touch a probe to each terminal. The needle should move to about 10 ohms. If the element has three terminals, touch one of the probes to the middle terminal, the other probe to each of the other two terminals. The meter should read about 20 ohms each time.

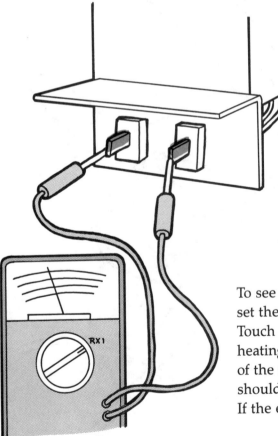

To see if the element has shorted to ground, set the volt-ohmmeter to the R×10 scale. Touch one probe to the bare metal of the heating duct and the other probe to each of the element's terminals. The meter needle should not move, indicating no connection. If the element fails any test, replace it.

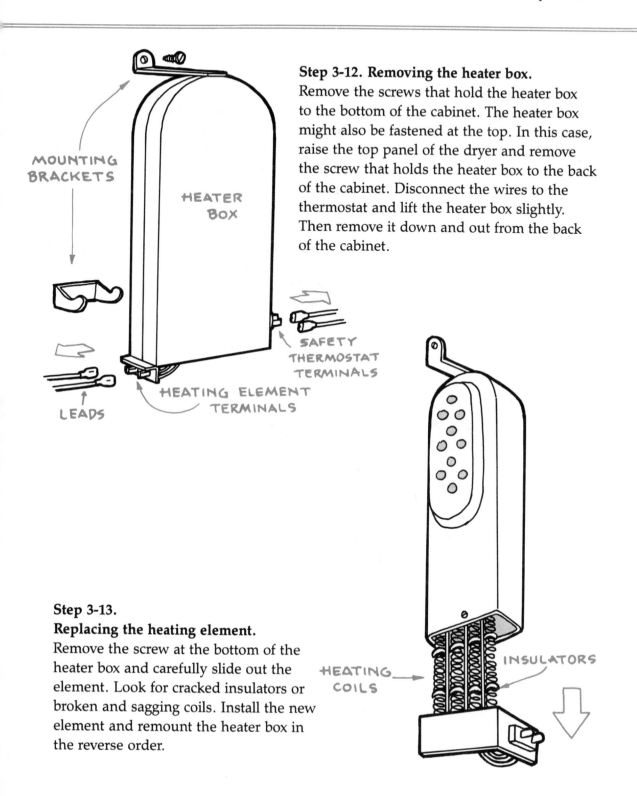

MOUNTING BRACKETS

HEATER BOX

SAFETY THERMOSTAT TERMINALS

HEATING ELEMENT TERMINALS

LEADS

Step 3-12. Removing the heater box.
Remove the screws that hold the heater box to the bottom of the cabinet. The heater box might also be fastened at the top. In this case, raise the top panel of the dryer and remove the screw that holds the heater box to the back of the cabinet. Disconnect the wires to the thermostat and lift the heater box slightly. Then remove it down and out from the back of the cabinet.

Step 3-13.
Replacing the heating element.
Remove the screw at the bottom of the heater box and carefully slide out the element. Look for cracked insulators or broken and sagging coils. Install the new element and remount the heater box in the reverse order.

HEATING COILS

INSULATORS

Step 3-14. Testing the heating coils.

If the dryer has heating coils mounted in a housing behind the drum, unplug the dryer and raise the top panel. Locate the coils' three terminals in the left rear of the cabinet. Label the wires and draw a wire diagram. Disconnect the wires from the terminals. Set the volt-ohmmeter to the R×1 scale. Touch one probe to the left (common) terminal and the other probe to each of the other two terminals.

In each test, the needle should move to about 5 or 10 ohms, showing continuity. To test if the element is shorted to ground, touch one probe to the heater housing and the other probe to each of the terminals. The needle should not move for any of these tests. If your results are different, replace both coils with new ones.

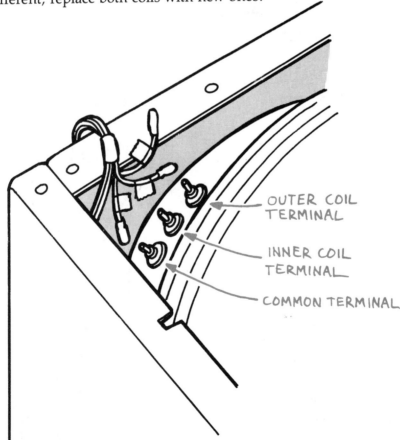

OUTER COIL TERMINAL

INNER COIL TERMINAL

COMMON TERMINAL

Step 3-15.

Preparing to remove the drum.

To replace the coils, you have to take out the drum. With the dryer unplugged, raise the top panel of the dryer. Remove the toe panel and the front panel from the dryer.

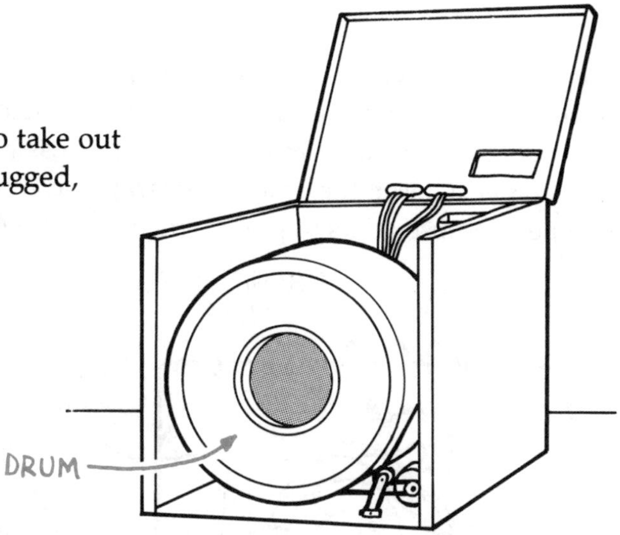

DRUM

Step 3-16.

Removing the drive belt.

Underneath the drum, push the idler pulley toward the motor and remove the belt from the motor pulley. Carefully lift the drum and slide it out from the front of the cabinet.

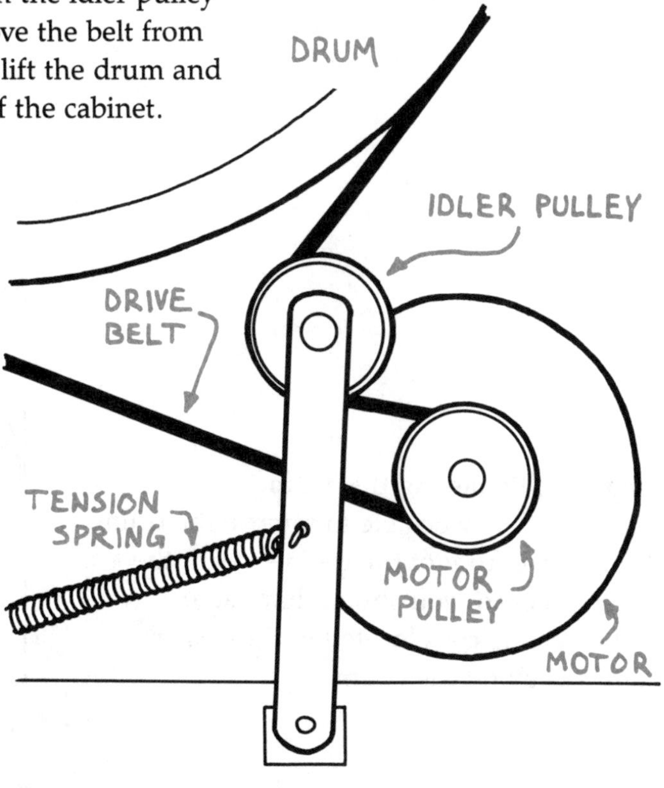

DRUM

IDLER PULLEY

DRIVE BELT

TENSION SPRING

MOTOR PULLEY

MOTOR

Step 3-17. Removing the retaining clip.
If the drum won't move, the shaft might be held by a retaining clip at
the rear of the drum. Remove the small access panel from the rear of
the cabinet. Loosen the grounding strap and move it out of the way.
Use needle-nose pliers to pry the retaining clip from the shaft.

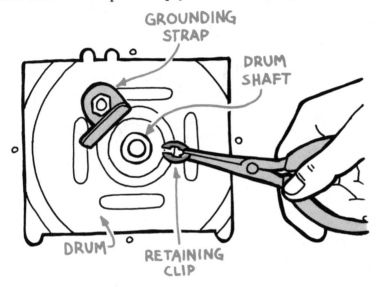

Step 3-18. Removing the drum.
You should now be able to remove the drum
through the front of the cabinet. With the
drum removed, you should have access
to the heating coils located in the heater
housing behind the drum.

Step 3-19. Removing the coils.

Look for breaks in the coils or insulators. Draw a wiring diagram
before removing the old coils. To remove the coils, use wire cutters
to cut the coils near the terminals. Gently remove the coils through
the insulators. The terminals are just threaded studs held in place by
nuts and washers. Use a small wrench to remove the nuts holding
the terminals to the heater housing. Keep the ceramic insulators,
but if the terminals are burned or corroded, install new ones.

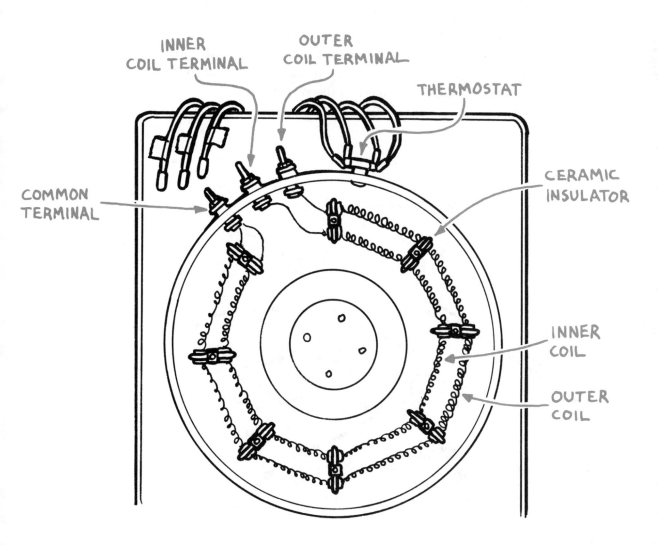

Step 3-20. Installing new coils.

Hook the end of the new coil around the terminal. Install another washer and nut so that the end of the coil is pressed tightly between two washers. Now place the ceramic insulator back on the terminal and mount the terminal in the hole on the heater housing. Install a terminal for the inside coil in the middle hole and the terminal for the outside coil in the right hand hole. Carefully thread the two coils clockwise through the proper insulators. Now connect the two free ends around the remaining terminal and install the terminal and insulators in the remaining hole. Reassemble the dryer in the reverse order.

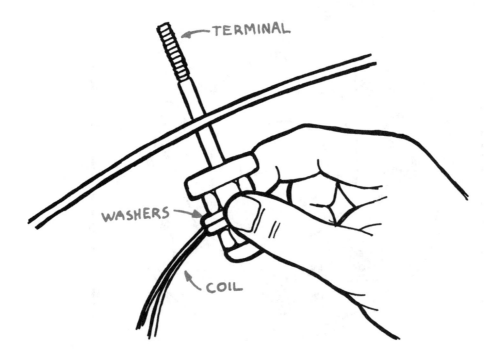

Step 3-21. Replacing drum drive belt.

Unplug the dryer. Depending on the dryer, you have to either remove the rear panel or remove the toe panel and raise the top panel of the dryer. Now remove the front panel.

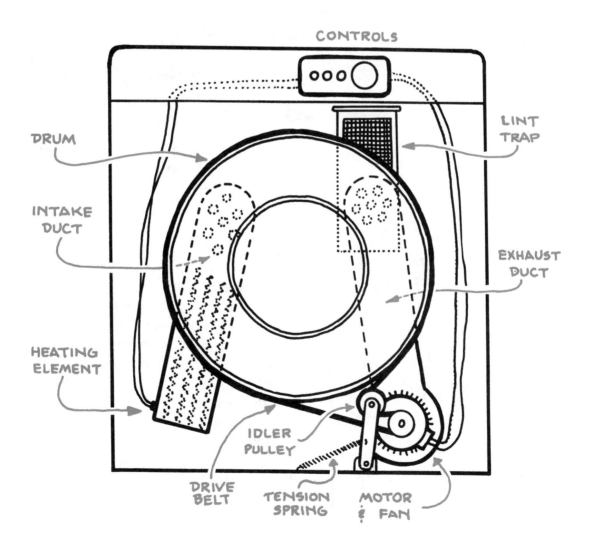

Step 3-22. Removing the belt.

Beneath the drum you should see the drive belt looped around the idler pulley and the motor pulley. Note how it is looped around the pulleys. Push the idler pulley toward the motor and disconnect the drive belt from the idler and motor pulleys.

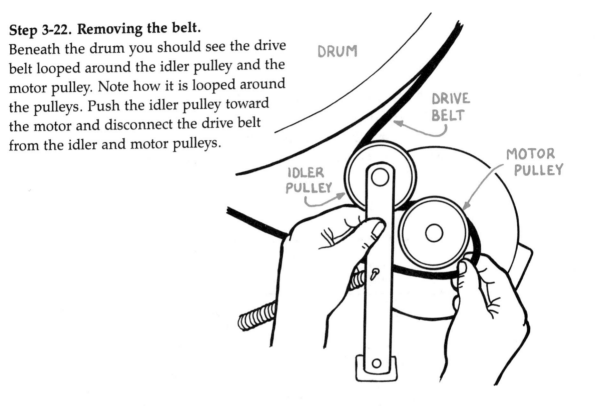

Step 3-23. Installing a new belt.

Lift the drum slightly and slide the old belt out the front of the cabinet. Install the new belt with the groove side down against the drum. Depending on the type of dryer, reconnect the drive belt under the idler pulley and over the motor pulley, or over the idler pulley and under the motor pulley, according to how the old one was looped. Now rotate the drum by hand to make sure the belt is properly installed. Reassemble the dryer.

CHAPTER FOUR

Refrigerators

A refrigerator is made up of a compressor, a condenser, an evaporator, and associated tubing and fans. Thermostats tell the different components when to operate. Normally, a fan pulls air over the evaporator, the evaporator chills the air, and the cold air is then pushed through ducts to cool the freezer and refrigerator compartments. The temperature controls tell the compressor when to operate. The refrigerator temperature control adjusts an air duct door that partially blocks the air flow into the refrigerator compartment, preventing the refrigerator compartment from getting as cold as the freezer compartment.

When frost builds up on the coils of the evaporator, the defrost cycle comes on, heating the coils to melt the frost. The water evaporates or is drained away to the drain pan.

Always unplug the refrigerator before making any repairs. Then wait about an hour before plugging it back in, to reduce the start-up strain on the compressor.

If you are replacing a door gasket, you'll need to know the make and model of the refrigerator. Many different types of door gaskets are available, and your parts supply store will probably have to order the one you need.

Tools & Materials

- [ ] Vacuum cleaner
- [ ] Screwdriver
- [ ] Adjustable wrench
- [ ] Small socket wrench and sockets
- [ ] Putty knife wrapped with masking tape
- [ ] Volt-ohmmeter or continuity tester
- [ ] Thermometer

EVAPORATOR COILS

EVAPORATOR FAN

DRIER-FILTER

CONDENSER FAN

COMPRESSOR

CONDENSER COILS

DE-FROST TIMER

DRAIN PAN

LIGHT SWITCH

TROUBLESHOOTING GUIDE

Problem	Probable causes	Solutions
Refrigerator doesn't run (light is out)	Power not reaching refrigerator	Make sure refrigerator is plugged in. Check for tripped circuit breaker.
Refrigerator doesn't run (light is on)	Temperature control faulty or in the OFF position	Check temperature control.
	Overheating compressor	Clean condenser coils. Check condenser fan.
	Defrost timer faulty or at defrost setting	Check defrost timer.
	Compressor relay faulty	Check compressor relay.
	Compressor overload protector faulty	Check compressor overload protector.
	Defective compressor	Check compressor.
Refrigerator runs but light is out	Burned out bulb	Replace bulb.
	Defective door switch	Check door switch.
Refrigerator runs but doesn't cool	Temperature control set too warm	Adjust temperature control to lower setting.
	Faulty temperature control	Check temperature control.
	Condenser coils covered with lint	Clean condenser coils.
	Faulty door gasket	Replace door gasket.
	Evaporator fan faulty	Check evaporator fan.
	Evaporator coated with ice	Defrost refrigerator. Check defrost timer.
Refrigerator too cold	Temperature control set too low	Adjust temperature to higher setting.
	Temperature control faulty	Check temperature control.
Refrigerator noisy	Refrigerator not level	Adjust leveling feet.
	Drain rattling	Reposition drain pan.
	Condenser fan faulty	Check condenser fan.

Step 4-1. Cleaning the condenser coils.

Unplug the refrigerator and pull it away from the
wall. Use a vacuum cleaner with a brush attachment
to remove dust and accumulated lint from the coils on
the back of the refrigerator. Remove the grill from the
bottom front of the refrigerator, and vacuum the area
behind the grill to remove accumulated dust and lint.

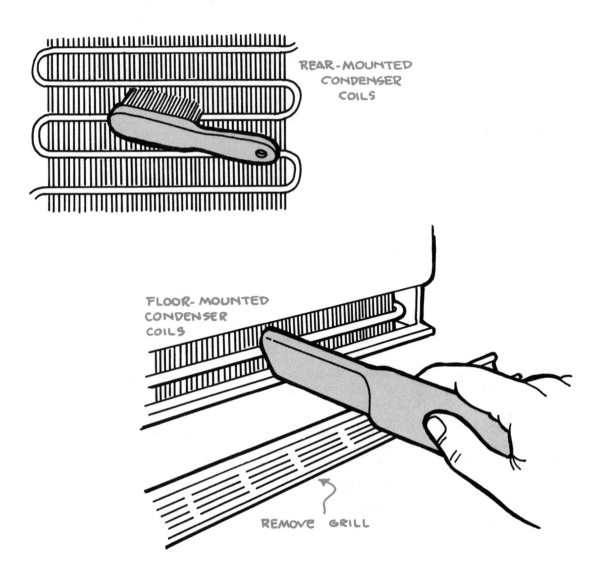

REAR-MOUNTED
CONDENSER
COILS

FLOOR-MOUNTED
CONDENSER
COILS

REMOVE GRILL

Step 4-2. Replacing a door gasket.

If the door gasket is brittle or has any cracks, replace it. If it is not damaged, close the door on a sheet of paper. You should feel tension when you pull the paper out. If you don't feel tension, the seal is not good—replace the gasket. Soak the new gasket in warm water to soften it. Then unplug the refrigerator and open the door. At the top of the door, pull back the old gasket to get to the retaining strip and screws. Use a small socket wrench or screwdriver to remove only the screws from the top edge of the door and the top two screws down each side. Remove the top section of the gasket and install the new one in its place.

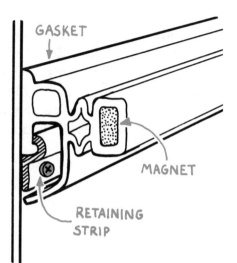

Step 4-3. Completing the job.

Install the gasket retaining strip and tighten the screws. Now repeat the procedure on the remaining three sides of the gasket, working one section at a time. Do not remove all the screws at one time. The door might warp out of shape.

Step 4-4.
Checking the light and door switch.
If the light does not come on when the door
is open, remove the old bulb and install a
new one with the same wattage. If the bulb
still does not light, check the door switch.

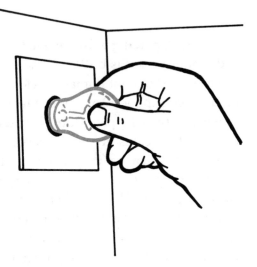

Step 4-5. Removing the door switch.
Unplug the refrigerator. Use a putty knife wrapped with a few turns
of masking tape to pry out the switch. Carefully pull out the switch
a few inches to get to the terminals. The switch might have one or
two pairs of terminals. Label the wires and draw a wiring diagram.
Now disconnect the wires from the terminals.

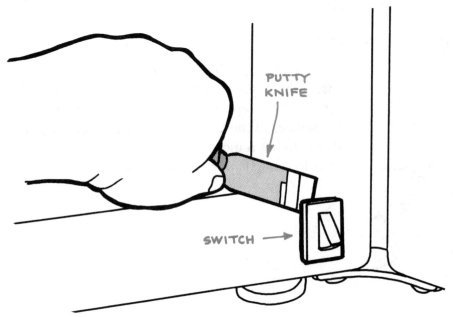

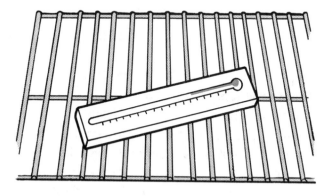

Step 4-6. Testing the door switch.
Use a volt-ohmmeter set on the R×1 scale or a
continuity tester to check for continuity. If the switch
has only two terminals, touch a probe to each terminal.
When the switch button is out, the needle should swing
to 0, showing continuity. Press the button in and the needle
should swing in the other direction, indicating no connection.
If the switch has four terminals, one pair of terminals should test
opposite the other pair. With the switch button out, one pair will
show continuity. With the switch button in, the other pair will show
continuity. If your switch tests differently, replace it with a new one.

Step 4-7.
Checking the temperature control.
Place a thermometer in the freezing compartment for a few minutes.
The temperature should be between 0 and 8 degrees F. Now check
the temperature in the refrigerator compartment. It should be
between 38 and 40 degrees F. If the temperature control fails to
produce the desired temperature, check the temperature control.

Step 4-8.
Removing the temperature control.
Unplug the refrigerator. If the control has a dial,
remove the dial, then the two screws holding the
control in place. Pull the control out just far enough
to get to the wires, being careful not to bend
the capillary (temperature-sensing) tube. If
the temperature control is behind a console,
remove the screws holding the console to
the wall of the refrigerator. The temperature
control will be attached to the console.

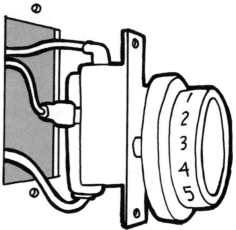

Step 4-9.
Testing the temperature control.
Now disconnect the two wires from
the terminals on the temperature control.
Using a volt-ohmmeter set on the R×1 scale
or a continuity tester, touch a probe to each
terminal of the control. When the control knob
is in the OFF position, the meter should not move.
With the control knob in the ON position or
any other setting, the meter should show
continuity (the needle should move).
Install a new temperature control
if the old one fails these tests.

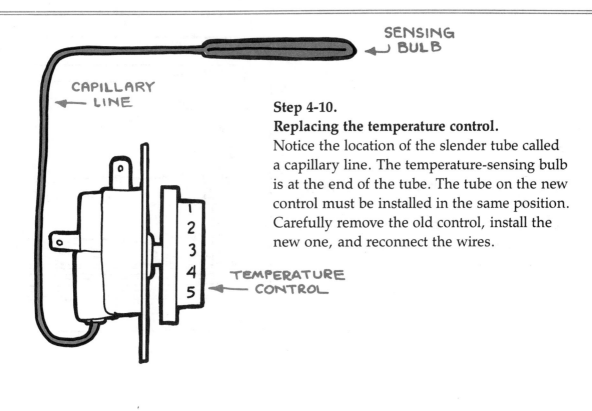

SENSING
BULB

CAPILLARY
LINE

Step 4-10.
Replacing the temperature control.
Notice the location of the slender tube called
a capillary line. The temperature-sensing bulb
is at the end of the tube. The tube on the new
control must be installed in the same position.
Carefully remove the old control, install the
new one, and reconnect the wires.

1
2
3
4
5

TEMPERATURE
CONTROL

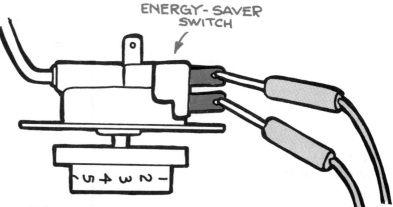

ENERGY-SAVER
SWITCH

Step 4-11.
Testing the energy-saver switch.
If the temperature control has an energy-saver switch, disconnect the
two wires from the switch and check it for continuity by touching a
probe to each terminal. If the switch is on, the meter should move to 0.
The meter should not move when the switch is off. If the switch fails
the tests, install a new one and reconnect the wires.

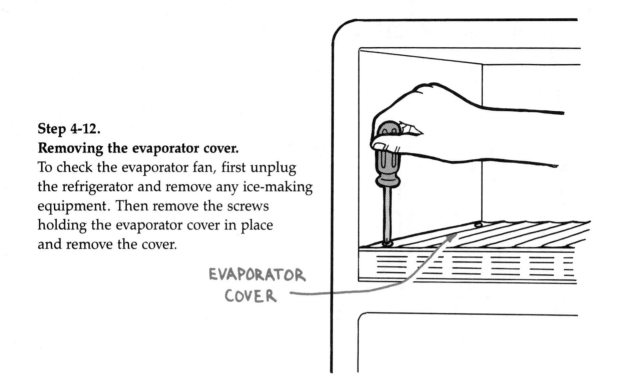

Step 4-12.
Removing the evaporator cover.
To check the evaporator fan, first unplug
the refrigerator and remove any ice-making
equipment. Then remove the screws
holding the evaporator cover in place
and remove the cover.

EVAPORATOR
COVER

Step 4-13.
Removing the insulation.
Beneath the cover you should find some
type of insulation or heat shield. Carefully
remove it from the compartment. You
should now have access to the fan.

Step 4-14. Removing the evaporator fan.

Remove the screws from each side of the fan's mounting bracket and carefully lift out the fan assembly. Now disconnect the two wires from the fan motor.

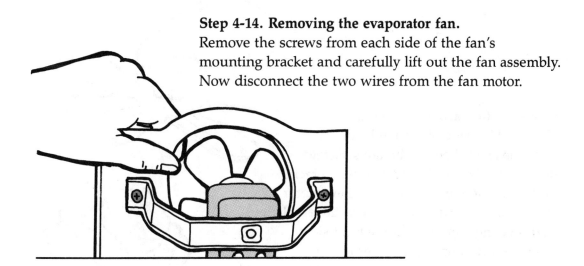

Step 4-15. Testing the fan motor.

Set the volt-ohmmeter to the R×1 scale and touch a probe to each of the two terminals. The meter should read about 150 ohms. If you get a higher reading or no reading at all, install a new motor. If the blade does not spin freely, install a new motor.

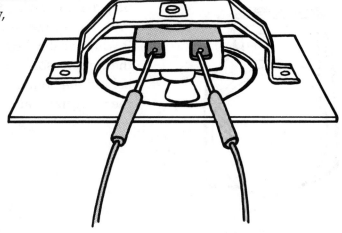

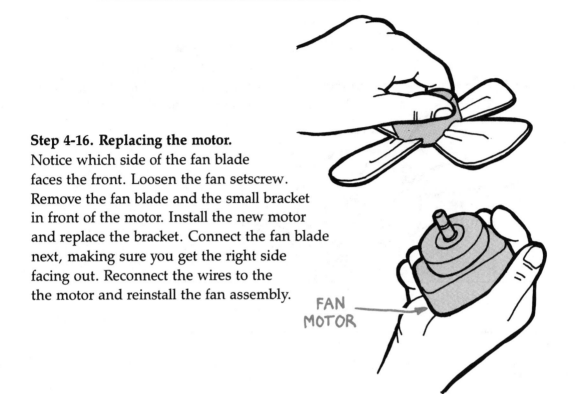

FAN
MOTOR

Step 4-16. Replacing the motor.
Notice which side of the fan blade
faces the front. Loosen the fan setscrew.
Remove the fan blade and the small bracket
in front of the motor. Install the new motor
and replace the bracket. Connect the fan blade
next, making sure you get the right side
facing out. Reconnect the wires to the
the motor and reinstall the fan assembly.

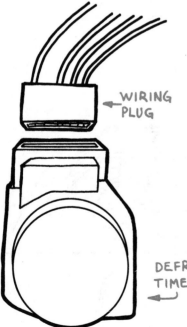

WIRING
PLUG

DEFROST
TIMER

Step 4-17. Locating the defrost timer.
With the refrigerator unplugged, locate the timer.
It will probably be at the back of the refrigerator in
the compressor compartment, but it also could be
behind the bottom front grill. Remove the timer from
the refrigerator and disconnect the wiring plug.

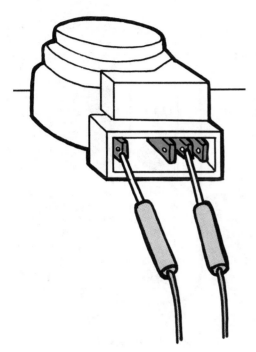

Step 4-18. Testing the defrost timer.
Set the volt-ohmmeter on the R×1 scale
and touch one probe to the terminal that
was connected to the white wire in the plug.
Touch the other probe to each of the other
three terminals. Two of the terminals should
show continuity while one will not.

Step 4-19. Performing the second test.
Use a screwdriver to turn the timer until it clicks,
and repeat the test. Again, two terminals will show
continuity and one will not, but this time they will
be different terminals. If the timer fails either test,
replace it with a new one.

Step 4-20. Replacing the defrost timer.
Use a screwdriver to remove the timer. Disconnect
any ground (green) wires, and unplug the wiring
plug from the timer. Reconnect the wiring plug to
the new timer and reconnect any ground wires.
Mount the new defrost timer to the refrigerator.

GROUND WIRES

TIMER

BACK OF REFRIGERATOR

Step 4-21. Checking the condenser fan.
While the refrigerator is running, remove the
front grill and feel for a draft of warm air from
the condenser fan motor. If you don't feel
any air blowing, unplug the refrigerator
and move it away from the wall.
Remove any rear access panels.
Spin the fan blade by hand. If
you feel any resistance, the
shaft is binding and the
motor must be replaced.

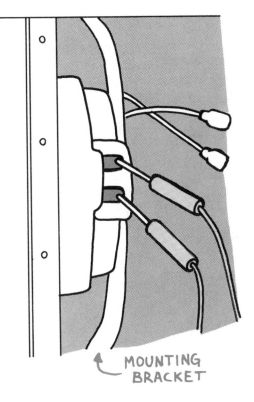

MOUNTING BRACKET

Step 4-22.
Testing the condenser fan motor.
Unplug the two wires to the terminals on the fan motor. With the volt-ohmmeter set on the R×10 scale, touch a probe to each of the two terminals on the fan motor. The needle should read around 75 to 150 ohms. A very high reading or no reading at all means the motor is faulty and needs to be replaced.

Step 4-23. Testing for a short.
Now set the volt-ohmmeter to the R×1K scale and touch one probe to any unpainted metal part of the refrigerator. Touch the other probe to each of the two terminals. If the needle moves at all, replace the motor.

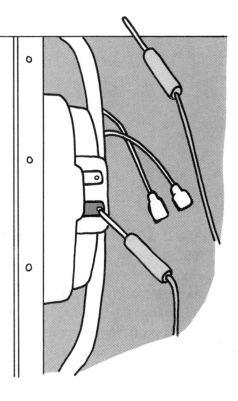

Step 4-24. Installing the new motor.
With the refrigerator unplugged and the wires disconnected
from the motor, disconnect the brackets that hold the motor in
place and remove the motor. Remove the fan blade from the old
motor and mount it on the new one. Mount the new motor in
the brackets and reconnect the wires to the motor terminals.

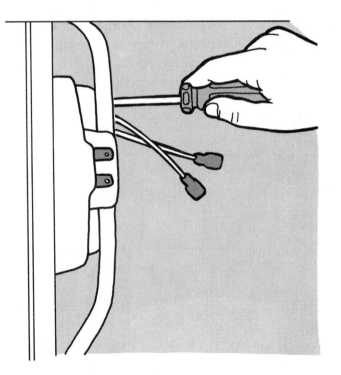

Step 4-25. Checking the compressor relay.
Unplug the refrigerator and move it away from the wall. Remove
any rear access panels. Locate the wires going into the compressor.
The connections might be protected by a cover held in place by
a spring clip. Remove the cover and you will see the relay and
overload protector. Some models might have a capacitor, which
looks like a small metal can with two terminals on one end.

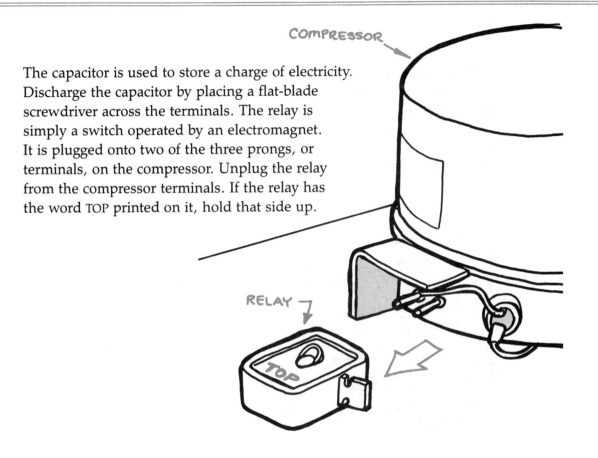

COMPRESSOR

RELAY

TOP

The capacitor is used to store a charge of electricity. Discharge the capacitor by placing a flat-blade screwdriver across the terminals. The relay is simply a switch operated by an electromagnet. It is plugged onto two of the three prongs, or terminals, on the compressor. Unplug the relay from the compressor terminals. If the relay has the word TOP printed on it, hold that side up.

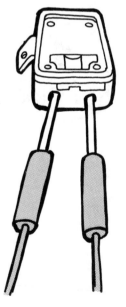

Step 4-26. Testing the relay.
Set the volt-ohmmeter to the R×1 scale. Touch one probe to the terminal marked S, and touch the other probe to the terminal marked M, then to the terminal marked L. The needle should not move. Now touch the probes to the terminals marked M and L. The needle should move to 0, showing continuity. Next, turn the relay upside down. You should hear a click. Repeat the test with the volt-ohmmeter. The readings should be the opposite of the first test. If your results differ, install a new relay. If the relay tests good, check the overload protector.

Step 4-27. Removing the overload protector.

You will see one wire plugged into a terminal on the overload protector and another wire from the overload protector connected to the remaining terminal on the compressor. Disconnect both of these wires. Now use a screwdriver to carefully release the spring clip holding the overload protector, and remove the overload protector from the compressor.

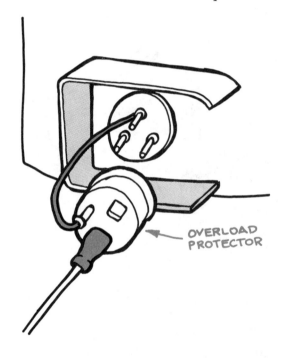

OVERLOAD
PROTECTOR

Step 4-28.

Testing the overload protector.

With the two wires disconnected, set the volt-ohmmeter to the R×1 scale. Touch a probe to each terminal on the overload protector. The needle should move to 0, showing continuity. If not, replace the overload protector with a new one. If the overload protector tests good, check the compressor.

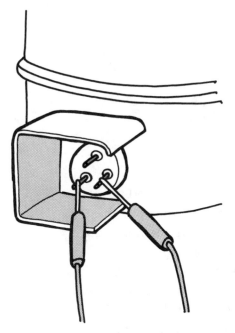

Step 4-29. Testing the compressor.
Set the volt-ohmmeter to the R×1 scale.
Touch one probe to one of the prongs,
or terminals, and the other probe to the
other two terminals, one at a time. Repeat
this test three times to cover all possible
combinations. You should find continuity
(the needle moves to 0) between any two
of the three compressor terminals.

Step 4-30. Testing for a short.
Now set the volt-ohmmeter to the R×1K scale.
Touch one probe to the bare metal of the compressor.
Touch the other probe to each of the three terminals in
turn. The needle should not move. If the needle does
move, indicating a connection with the metal frame,
for any of the three terminals, the compressor is
faulty and you should call for service.

CHAPTER FIVE

Ice Makers

Water enters an ice maker through an inlet valve and flows into the ice maker mold. The water is then frozen by the cold air in the freezer compartment. When the temperature in the mold has dropped to around 10 or 15 degrees, a thermostat starts a motor and the mold heater. The heater melts the ice slightly from below the mold, and the motor slowly drives the ejector blades clockwise to push the ice from the mold into the bin below. Next, the shutoff arm rises and the ejector blades return to their original position to start a new cycle. When the bin is full, the shutoff arm rests on the accumulated ice and stops the next cycle.

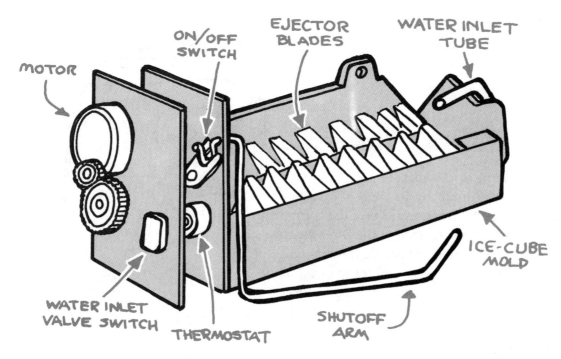

Tools & Materials

☐ Screwdriver
☐ Small socket wrench and sockets
☐ Kitchen knife
☐ Volt-ohmmeter or continuity tester
☐ Thermometer

TROUBLESHOOTING GUIDE

Problem	Probable causes	Solutions
Ice maker doesn't make ice	Water supply to ice maker shut off	Open water valve under sink or behind refrigerator.
	Freezer compartment too warm	Check temperature of freezing compartment—it must be no higher than 10° F.
	ON/OFF or holding switch faulty	Check ON/OFF switch and holding switch.
	Water inlet valve switch faulty	Check water inlet valve switch.
	Water inlet valve faulty	Check water inlet valve.
	Motor faulty	Check motor.
	Thermostat faulty	Check thermostat.
Ice maker doesn't stop making ice	Shutoff arm out of position	Reposition shutoff arm.
	ON/OFF switch faulty	Check ON/OFF switch.
Water overflows from ice maker	Ice maker not level	Adjust refrigerator leveling feet.
	Water inlet valve switch faulty	Check water inlet valve switch.
	Water inlet valve faulty	Check water inlet valve.
	Too much water delivered to ice cube mold	Adjust water adjustment screw.
Ice maker doesn't eject ice cubes	Motor faulty	Check motor.
	Holding switch faulty	Check holding switch.
	Thermostat faulty	Check thermostat.

Step 5-1. Removing the ice maker.
Unplug the refrigerator and remove the ice bin.
Use a screwdriver or small socket wrench to remove
the screw from the bottom bracket of the ice maker.

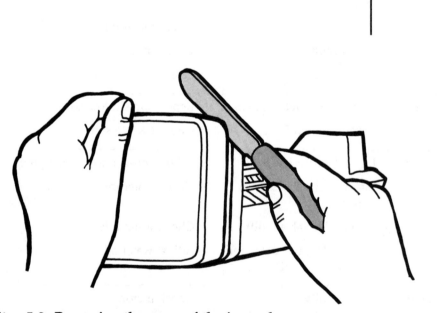

Step 5-2. Removing the cover of the ice maker.
Remove the top two screws and unplug the ice maker from the
refrigerator wall. Use the edge of a kitchen knife to pry off the cover.

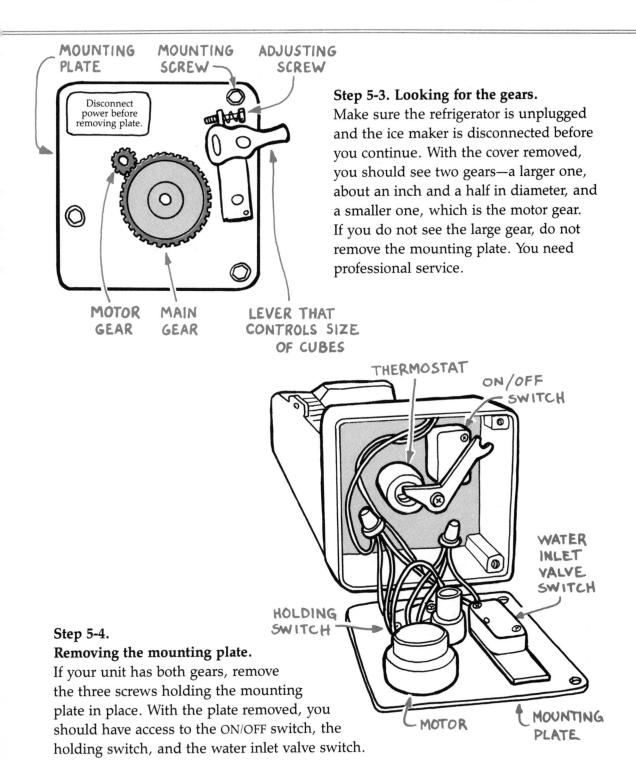

MOUNTING PLATE   MOUNTING SCREW   ADJUSTING SCREW

Disconnect power before removing plate.

MOTOR GEAR   MAIN GEAR   LEVER THAT CONTROLS SIZE OF CUBES

Step 5-3. Looking for the gears.

Make sure the refrigerator is unplugged and the ice maker is disconnected before you continue. With the cover removed, you should see two gears—a larger one, about an inch and a half in diameter, and a smaller one, which is the motor gear. If you do not see the large gear, do not remove the mounting plate. You need professional service.

THERMOSTAT   ON/OFF SWITCH

WATER INLET VALVE SWITCH

HOLDING SWITCH

MOTOR   MOUNTING PLATE

Step 5-4.
Removing the mounting plate.

If your unit has both gears, remove the three screws holding the mounting plate in place. With the plate removed, you should have access to the ON/OFF switch, the holding switch, and the water inlet valve switch.

Step 5-5. Testing the ON/OFF and holding switches.
Label the wires and disconnect them from all three of the switches.
The ON/OFF and holding switches have three terminals, but the water
inlet valve switch has only two. Set the volt-ohmmeter to the R×1 scale
or use a continuity tester. Touch one probe to the common terminal
located on the side of the ON/OFF switch and the other probe to each
of the two terminals on the end. The meter should
show continuity at one terminal and not at the
other. Press in the button on the switch and
repeat the test. The results should be the
opposite. If the switch fails either test,
replace it with a new one. Check the
holding switch the same way.

Step 5-6. Testing the water inlet valve switch.
Using a volt-ohmmeter set on the R×1 scale or a
continuity tester, touch one probe to each of the
two terminals. With the button out, the needle
should move to 0, showing continuity. With the
button in, the needle should not move. If not,
install a new water inlet valve switch. You will
notice that this switch has an insulating disk
between it and the mounting plate. Reinstall
this insulator when replacing the switch.

Shopping List for All Thumbs Guide
to Repairing Major Home Appliances

VOLT - OHMMETER

CONTINUITY TESTER

NEEDLE-NOSE PLIERS

SLIP-JOINT PLIERS

FLAT - BLADE SCREWDRIVER

PHILLIPS SCREWDRIVER

WIRE CUTTERS

ADJUSTABLE WRENCH

PIPE WRENCH

PUTTY KNIFE

ELECTRICAL TAPE

MASKING TAPE

- ☐ Volt-ohmmeter
- ☐ Continuity tester
- ☐ Needle-nose pliers
- ☐ Slip-joint pliers
- ☐ Standard flat-blade screwdrivers ($\frac{1}{8}$-, $\frac{3}{16}$-, $\frac{1}{4}$-, $\frac{5}{16}$-inch tips)
- ☐ Medium Phillips screwdriver
- ☐ Small Phillips screwdriver
- ☐ Wire cutters
- ☐ Adjustable wrench
- ☐ Pipe wrench
- ☐ Putty knife
- ☐ Flashlight
- ☐ Electrical tape
- ☐ Masking tape
- ☐ _____
- ☐ _____
- ☐ _____
- ☐ _____
- ☐ _____

Refer to the lists at the beginning of the chapters
for the tools you need for individual projects.

Safety Tips

Before you start:

○ Think safety.

○ Work slowly and carefully.

○ Read and understand all instructions.

○ Gather all your tools and required materials.

○ Make sure your test equipment is working properly.

○ Make absolutely certain that no voltage is present when you are working around water.

○ Never work on any live circuit, fixture, or appliance.

○ Turn off the power or unplug the appliance.

○ Use your test equipment to confirm that the power is off.

○ If you have any doubt that the power to a circuit is off, turn off the main breaker.

○ Make sure that no one will restore the power while you are working. One way to do this is to tag the breaker with a notice reading "Danger! Do not reset."

○ Make sure you know the procedures to follow if a person comes in contact with a live circuit. If someone has been shocked and is still part of the live circuit, don't touch him or her with your bare hands. First try to disconnect the power. If you cannot, use some type of insulated device, such as a coat or broom, to remove the victim from the circuit. Keep the victim warm while you call for help. You might need to perform artificial respiration.

From All Thumbs Guide to *Repairing Major Home Appliances* by Robert W. Wood.
© 1992 by TAB Books, a division of McGraw-Hill, Inc.

Step 5-7. Checking the motor.
With the refrigerator unplugged, and
the ice maker and the mounting plate
removed, disconnect the wires to the
motor. Set the volt-ohmmeter to
the R×10 scale. Now touch a
probe to the bare end of each
wire. The needle should move to
about 500 ohms. If the needle does not
move, the motor is bad and needs to be
replaced. To replace the motor, simply remove
the screws holding the motor to the mounting plate. Install the new
motor by fitting the motor gear into the large gear on the mounting
plate, reinstalling the screws, and reconnecting the wires.

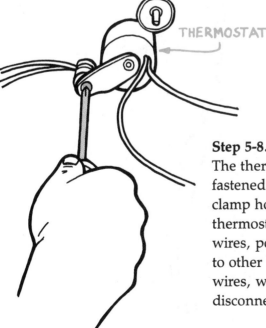

THERMOSTAT

Step 5-8. Removing the thermostat.
The thermostat is held in place by a clamp
fastened by a screw. Remove the screw and
clamp holding the thermostat. Then remove the
thermostat. The thermostat will have at least two
wires, possibly three. One wire will be connected
to other wires by a wire nut. The other wire, or
wires, will have terminal connectors. Label and
disconnect the wires to the thermostat.

Step 5-9. Testing the thermostat.

Set the volt-ohmmeter to the R×1 scale. If the thermostat has three wires, touch one probe to the shorter of the two wires with terminal connectors. Touch the other probe to each of the other two wires. The meter should show continuity to one wire and not to the other. For the next test, the thermostat must be chilled. If you have access to another freezer, place the thermostat in that freezer for about 20 minutes; then repeat the test. The results should be the opposite of those in the first test. If your thermostat has only two wires, it should show continuity when cold, at 10 degrees F or below, and no continuity when warm. If the thermostat fails the test, install a new one. Reconnect the wires and reassemble the ice maker in reverse order.

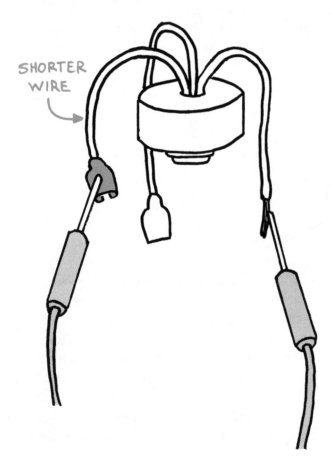

SHORTER
WIRE

Step 5-10. Disconnecting the water inlet valve.
Turn off the water supply valve, which you will
find either behind the refrigerator or under the
sink. Unplug the refrigerator and pull it away
from the wall. Disconnect both tubes from
the water inlet valve openings. Disconnect
the water inlet valve from the back of the
refrigerator. Now disconnect the wiring
plugs and any ground (green) wires.

Step 5-11. Testing the water inlet valve.
Set the volt-ohmmeter to the R×10 scale and touch a probe
to each terminal. The needle should move to about 300 ohms.
If the needle doesn't move, install a new inlet valve. If the
needle moves, clean the filter on the inlet side of the valve.
Reconnect the wiring plugs and connect the ground wire.
Remount the valve on the back of the
refrigerator and reconnect the tubes
to the valve openings. Turn the water
supply valve back on and check for any leaks.

CHAPTER SIX

Dishwashers

A typical cycle on a dishwasher begins when you close and latch the door, push a cycle selector button, and turn on the timer. The timer opens the water inlet valve, allowing hot water to flow into the tub. Detergent released by the detergent dispenser mixes with the hot water, which is further heated by a heating element. The timer then turns on the motor attached to the pump. The pump pushes the water through a spray arm that spins, spraying the hot soapy water onto the dishes. When the timer reaches the end of the wash or rinse cycle, the motor pumps the water out of the dishwasher and into the house drain. With the tub empty, the heating element dries the dishes as the timer reaches the OFF position, completing the cycle.

The most common complaint about a dishwasher is that the dishes are not getting clean. There are a number of possible causes. The detergent dispenser might not be releasing the detergent, the detergent might not be right for your type of water, the dishwasher might not be getting enough water, or the water might not be hot enough. Dishwashers are complicated machines, but most problems can be repaired easily by the homeowner. The one area that should be left to a professional is the pump and motor assembly. If the pump seal is not properly installed, water can leak into the motor, creating many more problems than you started with. Before beginning any repairs, make sure the power is turned off. If you find that the parts are inaccessible, call a professional.

Tools & Materials

- ☐ Screwdriver
- ☐ Volt-ohmmeter or continuity tester
- ☐ Pliers
- ☐ Adjustable wrench
- ☐ Shallow pan or towel
- ☐ Old toothbrush
- ☐ Stiff wire

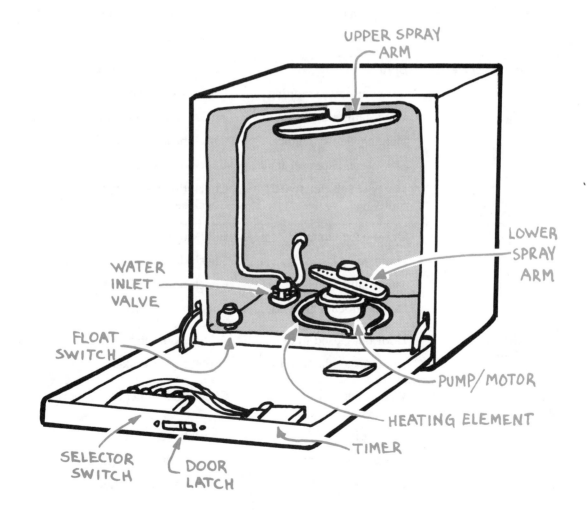

UPPER SPRAY ARM

LOWER SPRAY ARM

WATER INLET VALVE

FLOAT SWITCH

PUMP/MOTOR

HEATING ELEMENT

TIMER

SELECTOR SWITCH

DOOR LATCH

TROUBLESHOOTING GUIDE

Problem	Probable causes	Solutions
Dishwasher doesn't run	No power to dishwasher	Check circuit breaker.
	Door not latched or door switch faulty	Latch door. Check door switch.
	Timer faulty	Check timer and timer motor.
Dishwasher doesn't fill or overfills with water	Faulty float switch	Check float switch.
	Faulty water inlet valve	Check water inlet valve.
	Faulty timer	Check timer and timer motor.
Dishes don't get clean	Spray arm clogged	Clean holes in spray arm.
	Spray arm not spinning	Check spray arm for rotation.
	Water temperature too low	Adjust water heater setting.
	Heating element faulty	Check heating element.
	Detergent dispenser faulty	Check detergent dispenser.
	Timer or selector switch faulty	Check timer and timer motor. Check selector switch.
Water doesn't drain	Drain hose kinked	Check drain hose.
	Drain valve faulty	Check drain valve.
	Timer faulty	Check timer and timer motor.
	Pump impeller clogged	Call repair service.
Dishwasher leaks around door	Door not closed tight	Adjust door latch.
	Door gasket damaged	Replace door gasket.
Dishwasher leaks from bottom	Water inlet valve connection loose	Check water inlet connection.
	Hose split	Check hoses.
	Broken spray arm	Check spray arm.
	Faulty pump seal	Call for repair service.

Step 6-1. Removing the door panel.

Turn off the power to the dishwasher at the service entrance panel. Open the door and remove the screws along the inside edge of the door. These screws hold the door panel in place. Now remove the door panel from the front of the door.

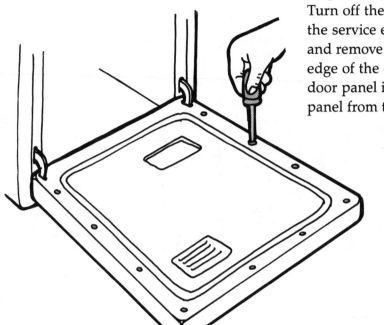

Step 6-2.
Unscrewing the control panel.

Now remove the screws around the top inside edge of the door. These screws hold the control panel in place. Support the control panel with one hand to keep it from falling.

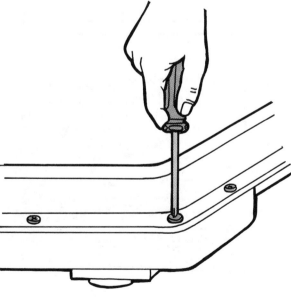

Step 6-3. Removing the control panel.
Close the door and lower the control panel,
being careful not to damage or strain the wires.

Step 6-4. Gaining access to the controls.
You should now have access to the timer, door switch,
selector switch, wiring diagram, and detergent dispenser.

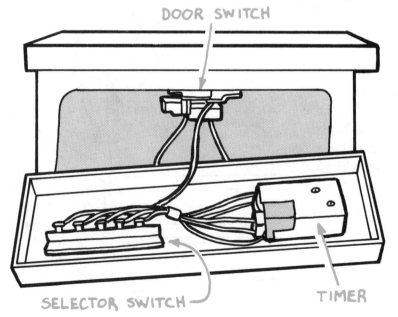

Step 6-5. Testing the timer motor.

Unplug the wires going to the timer motor.
Set a volt-ohmmeter on the R×1 scale.
Place one probe on one of the wires and
the other probe on the other wire. The
needle should move, showing continuity.
If not, the motor is faulty and the entire
timer will have to be replaced. If the motor
checks okay, check the timer.

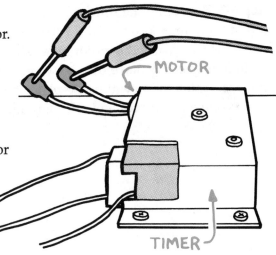

Step 6-6. Testing the timer.

Disconnect the wiring plug from the timer terminals. Now consult the
wiring diagram on the back of the door panel. Set the volt-ohmmeter
to the R×1 scale and touch a probe to each terminal of the first cycle.
The needle should move to 0, showing continuity. Turn the timer
dial to the next step in the cycle. Touch the probes to the terminals
connected to that step in the cycle. Again, the needle should
show continuity. Continue turning the dial and checking
the terminals until you go through the full cycle.
If any pair of terminals fails to show continuity,
the timer should be replaced.

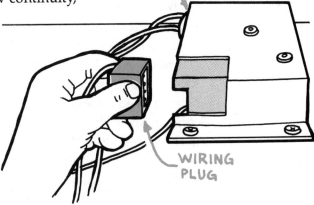

Step 6-7. Replacing the timer.

Remove the timer knob from the front of the panel.
The wiring plug and the motor wires should already
be disconnected. Remove the screws holding the timer
in place. Install the new timer, replace the knob,
and reconnect the wires and wiring plug.

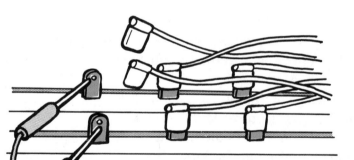

Step 6-8. Checking the cycle selector switches.

With the power disconnected and the control panel removed,
set the volt-ohmmeter to the R×1 scale. Now disconnect the two
wires to the terminals of the first switch. Press that switch to the
ON position and connect the probes to the two terminals. The
needle should swing to 0, showing continuity. With the switch
off, the needle should swing in the other direction, indicating no
connection. If that switch checks okay, reconnect the two wires
to the terminals and go to the next switch. Repeat the steps until
you have tested all the switches. If any switch fails to show
continuity, replace that switch.

Step 6-9. Replacing a cycle selector switch.
Remove the screws holding the switch bracket to the control panel. Remove the push button from the faulty switch. Remove the screws holding the switch in place. Install a new switch. Replace the push button and reconnect the wires to the terminals. Then reinstall the bracket on the control panel.

DOOR SWITCH

DOOR LATCH

Step 6-10. Checking the door switch.
With the power off and the control panel removed, close and latch the door. Now disconnect the two wires from the door switch terminal. Set the volt-ohmmeter on the $R \times 1$ scale and touch a probe to each of the terminals. The needle should swing to 0, showing continuity. With the door unlatched, the meter should indicate no continuity. If the switch fails these tests, install a new one.

Step 6-11. Installing the door switch.

With the wires disconnected, remove the screws holding the switch to the door panel. Mount the new one in the door panel. Connect the wires to the terminal of the new switch.

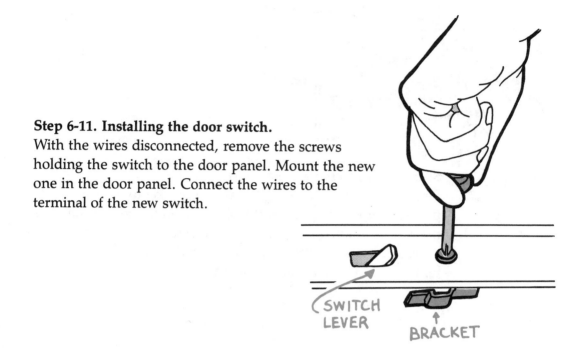

SWITCH LEVER

BRACKET

Step 6-12. Checking the detergent dispenser.

Work the detergent dispenser arm back and forth by hand to make sure it doesn't stick. Replace any damaged parts.

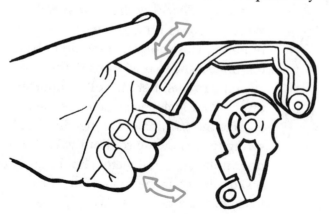

Step 6-13. Removing the lower front panel.

With the power to the dishwasher off, remove any screws
holding the lower front panel in place. Pull the panel down and
lift it away from the front of the machine. Now you should have
access to the water inlet valve, the drain valve, the pump and
motor assembly, the terminals to the heating element, and the
terminals to the float switch. The float switch probably is
positioned near the bottom of the tub and might be hard to see.

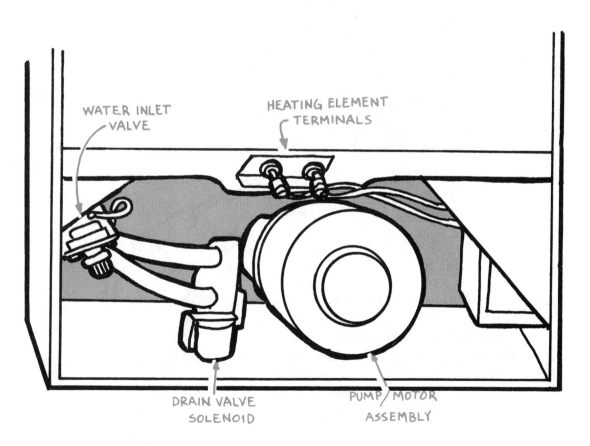

WATER INLET
VALVE

HEATING ELEMENT
TERMINALS

DRAIN VALVE
SOLENOID

PUMP/MOTOR
ASSEMBLY

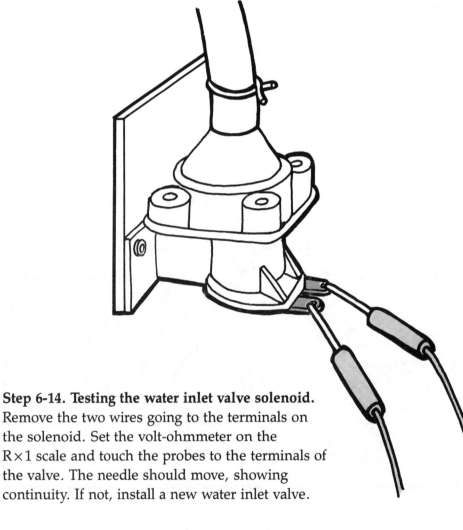

Step 6-14. Testing the water inlet valve solenoid.
Remove the two wires going to the terminals on
the solenoid. Set the volt-ohmmeter on the
R×1 scale and touch the probes to the terminals of
the valve. The needle should move, showing
continuity. If not, install a new water inlet valve.

Step 6-15. Removing and replacing the water inlet valve.

Before removing the water inlet valve, shut off the hot water supply valve under the sink. Place a shallow pan or an old towel under the inlet valve to catch any spilled water. Use pliers to disconnect the hose from the valve to the tub. Use an adjustable wrench to disconnect the water supply hose from the valve. With the wires disconnected, remove the screws that hold the valve to the machine. If the old valve tested okay, pry out the screen and clean it with an old toothbrush. Place the screen back in the valve and reinstall the old valve. If the old valve failed the test, install a new one. Reconnect the water line and the wires.

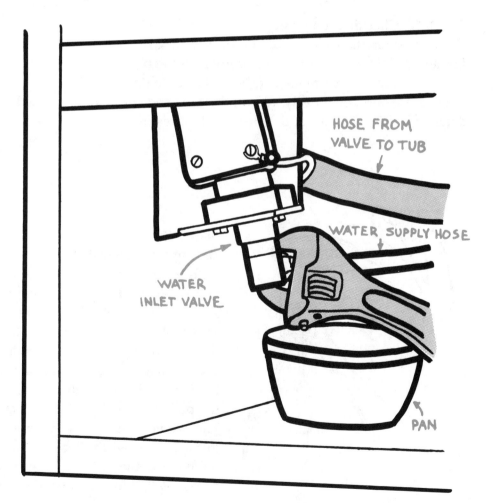

FLOAT COVER

FLOAT

Step 6-16. Checking the float.
Open the door and slide out the lower dish rack.
Locate the float in one of the front corners of the tub.
If the float has a cover, remove it. Now check the float to make sure
it moves up and down freely. Lift off the float and check for any caked
detergent. If the float is not damaged and moves freely, reinstall the float.

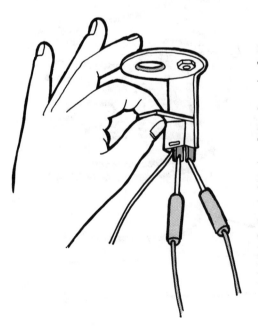

Step 6-17.
Testing the float switch.
With the lower panel removed, look at the
area directly below the float in the tub. You
should see two wires going to a switch.
This switch is the float switch. Disconnect
the two wires going to the terminals of the
float switch. Using a volt-ohmmeter set to
the $R \times 1$ scale or a continuity tester, touch
the probes to the terminals of the switch.
The needle should show continuity. If not,
install a new switch. Remove the screws
holding the switch in place, install the
new switch, and reconnect the wires.

Step 6-18. Checking for a drain valve.

With the lower panel removed, count the number of wires going to the motor. If you see four wires, the motor is reversible and does not have a drain valve. If you see only two or three wires, the motor is nonreversible and should have a drain valve.

Step 6-19. Testing the drain valve solenoid.

Locate the drain valve near the pump and motor assembly. Disconnect the two wires going to the terminals on the drain valve solenoid. Set the volt-ohmmeter on the R×1 scale and touch the probes to each of the two terminals. The needle should move, showing continuity. If not, install a new solenoid.

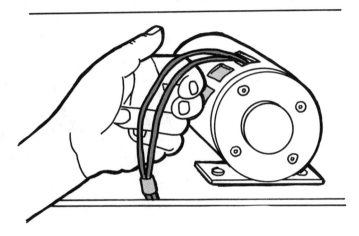

SOLENOID

SPRING

Step 6-20. Replacing the solenoid.
With the wires disconnected, remove the
screws holding the solenoid to the valve.
Disconnect any springs, install the new
solenoid, and reconnect the springs.
Mount the new solenoid on the valve
and reconnect the wires.

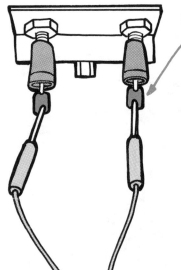

HEATING ELEMENT
TERMINAL

Step 6-21. Checking the heating element.
With the power turned off and the lower panel
removed, locate the two wires going to the
heating element. Disconnect the two wires
going to the heating element terminals. Set a
volt-ohmmeter on the R×1 scale and touch
a probe to each of the two terminals. The
needle should move, showing continuity.
If not, install a new element.

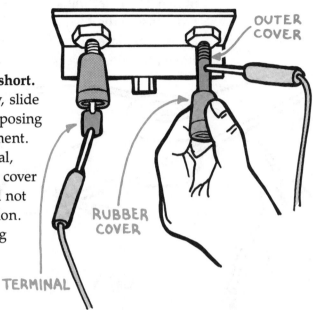

Step 6-22.
Testing the heating element for a short.
If the heating element checks okay, slide down one of the rubber covers, exposing the outer cover of the heating element. With one probe touching a terminal, touch the other probe to the outer cover of the element. The needle should not move at all, indicating no connection. If it does move, replace the heating element with a new one.

OUTER COVER

RUBBER COVER

TERMINAL

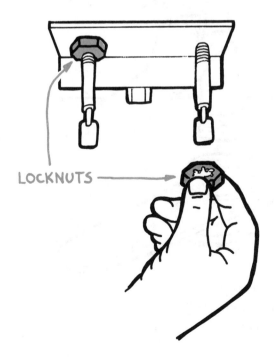

LOCKNUTS

Step 6-23.
Removing the heating element.
With the wires disconnected, remove the rubber terminal covers and unscrew the locknuts that hold the element in place.

Step 6-24. Installing a new element.
From inside the tub, remove the element and install an exact replacement. Then reinstall the locknuts and rubber terminal covers and reconnect the wires.

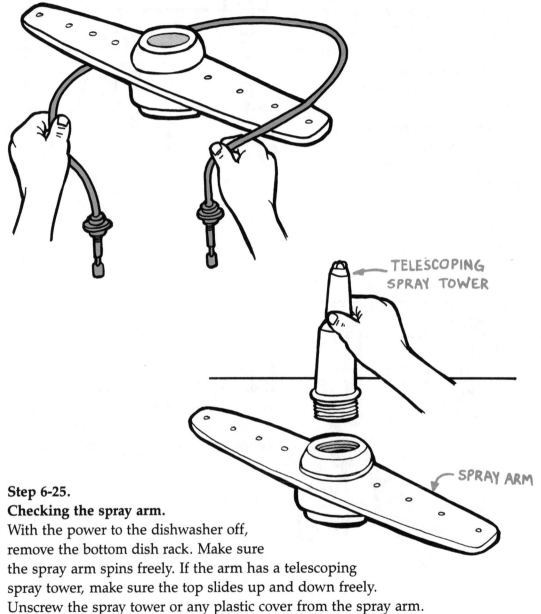

TELESCOPING SPRAY TOWER

SPRAY ARM

Step 6-25.
Checking the spray arm.
With the power to the dishwasher off,
remove the bottom dish rack. Make sure
the spray arm spins freely. If the arm has a telescoping
spray tower, make sure the top slides up and down freely.
Unscrew the spray tower or any plastic cover from the spray arm.

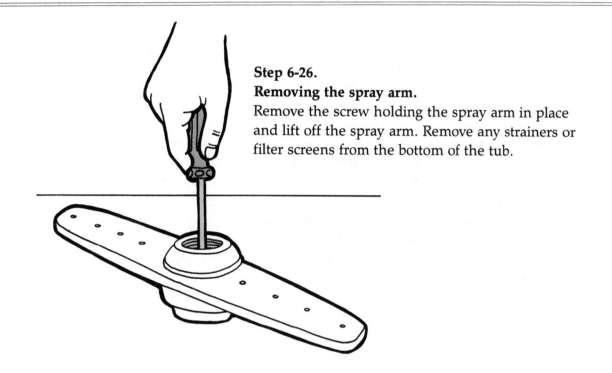

Step 6-26.
Removing the spray arm.
Remove the screw holding the spray arm in place and lift off the spray arm. Remove any strainers or filter screens from the bottom of the tub.

Step 6-27. Cleaning the spray arm.
Unclog the holes on both sides of the spray arm with a stiff wire. Next rinse the spray arm, strainer, and screen under running water. Scrub the screen and strainer with an old toothbrush. Reassemble the parts in the reverse order.

Step 6-28. Replacing the door gasket.

Depending on the type of dishwasher, the gasket might be in the
tub opening or on the door. The gasket might be held in place with
screws or with clips that can be pried off with a screwdriver. Soak
the new gasket in warm water to remove any kinks. Remove the old
gasket and place the center of the new gasket at the center of the top
of the door. Fasten several inches of the gasket in place at the top of
the door. Working around the door a few inches at a time, continue
fastening the new gasket in place. Once the new gasket is in place,
make sure the door latch closes the door securely. Often the latch
can be repositioned by loosening the screws, adjusting the latch,
and then tightening the screws.

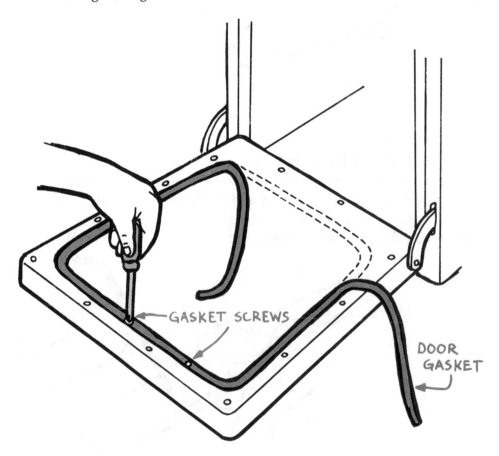

GASKET SCREWS

DOOR
GASKET

CHAPTER SEVEN

Electric Ranges

Electric ranges come in a variety of sizes and shapes, but they all work in pretty much the same way. They operate on a 120/240-volt circuit. Typically, 120 volts are used for the light and clock, 240 volts for the heating elements. However, some older models might have heating elements made of two coils controlled by a switch that applies either 120 or 240 volts to either or both of the coils, depending on the heat setting. Newer ranges usually have single-coil elements operated by a thermostatically controlled switch. These switches smoothly regulate the temperature from low to high, and at any point in between. Self-cleaning ovens use a cycle that raises the temperature of the oven to about 900 degrees F. This high temperature burns off any cooking residues from the oven walls. An automatic safety door lock prevents the oven door from being opened until the cleaning cycle ends and the oven temperature lowers to about 300 degrees.

Before making any repairs, always turn off the power at the service entrance panel. Let heating elements cool completely before touching them. Always open and close the range's lift-up cook top carefully to avoid straining any wires.

When making some of the tests, you need to refer to the wiring diagram provided by the manufacturer. You should find it stuck on the inside of the control or back panel, depending on the type of range you have.

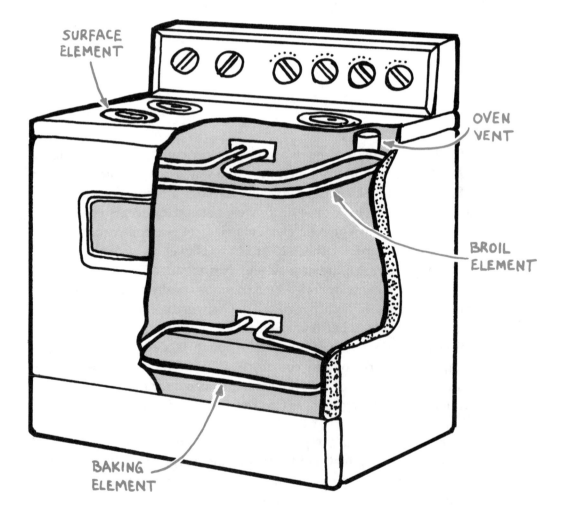

SURFACE ELEMENT

OVEN VENT

BROIL ELEMENT

BAKING ELEMENT

Tools & Materials

- ☐ Steel wool
- ☐ Volt-ohmmeter or continuity tester
- ☐ Emery board
- ☐ Screwdriver
- ☐ Needle-nose pliers
- ☐ Gloves and goggles, if necessary
- ☐ Oven thermometer
- ☐ 40-watt bulb

TROUBLESHOOTING GUIDE

Problem	Probable cause	Solutions
No elements heat; lights are out	No power to range	Check for tripped circuit breaker.
One cooktop element doesn't heat	Faulty element	Check element.
	Element receptacle faulty	Check element receptacle.
	Burner switch faulty	Check burner switch.
Oven doesn't heat	Faulty oven element	Check element.
	Automatic timer improperly set	Reset timer to manual.
	Faulty oven temperature control	Check oven temperature control.
	Faulty oven selector switch	Check oven selector switch.
Oven doesn't maintain set temperature	Oven temperature control improperly calibrated	Check and recalibrate oven temperature control.
Oven light out	Bulb burned out	Replace bulb.
	Faulty light switch	Check light switch.

Step 7-1. Checking a top element.
First turn off the power to the range. Then lift the edge of the
element just enough to clear the drip pan. Pull the element
straight out. Use steel wool to polish any corroded terminals
on the element. Remove another element of the same size
that works properly, and plug the suspect element into the
receptacle of the working element. Restore power to the
range and turn on the burner. If the suspect element does
not heat now, replace it with a new one. If the element does
heat, check the element's terminal receptacle. If the range
does not have another element that is the same size, check
the suspect element with a volt-ohmmeter (Step 7-2).

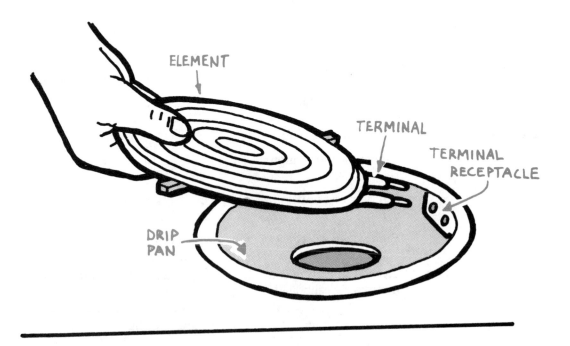

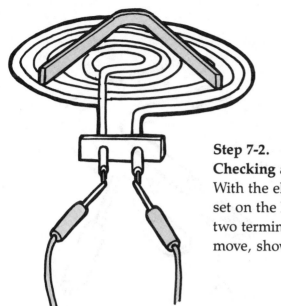

Step 7-2.
Checking a burner element with a volt-ohmmeter.
With the element unplugged and the volt-ohmmeter set on the R×1 scale, touch a probe to each of the two terminals of the element. The needle should move, showing continuity.

Step 7-3. Testing the element's terminals.
If the heating element has two separate coils, it should have three terminals—one common terminal connecting the two coils together and two individual terminals on the other ends of the coils. Touch one probe to the common terminal and the other probe to each of the other two terminals. In each case the needle should swing, indicating continuity. If not, replace the heating element with a new one.

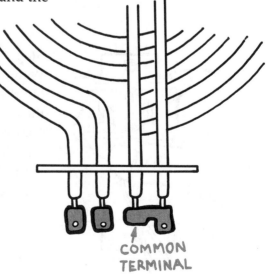

COMMON
TERMINAL

Step 7-4.
Testing the element for a short.
If the element checks as good, touch one probe to one of the terminals and the other probe to the outer metal cover of the element. The needle should not move, indicating no continuity. If the needle does move, the element is shorted. Replace it with a new one.

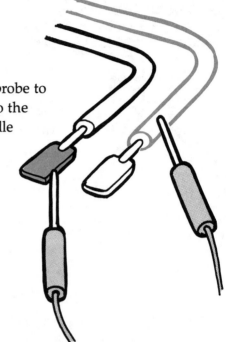

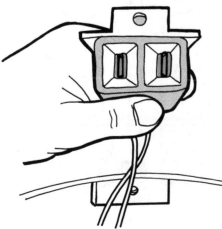

Step 7-5. Checking the element receptacle.
With the power off and the element removed, lift out the drip pan. Disconnect the receptacle from the top of the stove and carefully pull it out for inspection. Check the slots that the element plugs into. If the slots are dirty, polish them carefully with a thin fingernail emery board. If the slots are charred or broken, install a new receptacle.

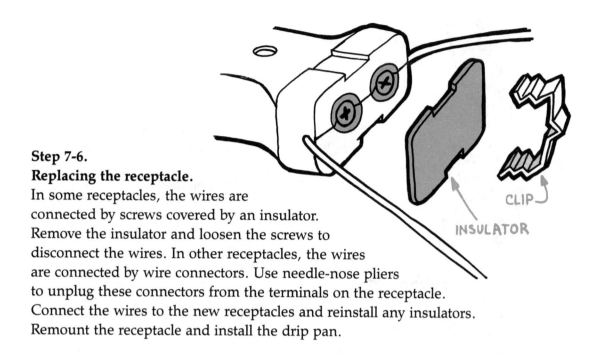

Step 7-6.
Replacing the receptacle.
In some receptacles, the wires are
connected by screws covered by an insulator.
Remove the insulator and loosen the screws to
disconnect the wires. In other receptacles, the wires
are connected by wire connectors. Use needle-nose pliers
to unplug these connectors from the terminals on the receptacle.
Connect the wires to the new receptacles and reinstall any insulators.
Remount the receptacle and install the drip pan.

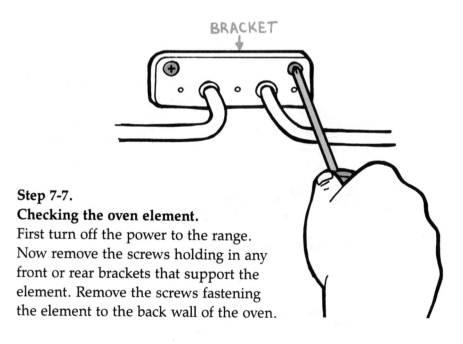

Step 7-7.
Checking the oven element.
First turn off the power to the range.
Now remove the screws holding in any
front or rear brackets that support the
element. Remove the screws fastening
the element to the back wall of the oven.

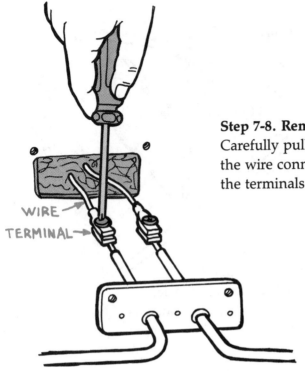

WIRE
TERMINAL

Step 7-8. Removing the oven element.
Carefully pull the element out a few inches to expose the wire connections. Disconnect the two wires from the terminals. Remove the element.

Step 7-9. Testing the oven element.
Set the volt-ohmmeter on the R×1 scale and touch a probe to each of the two terminals. The needle should move, showing continuity. If not, install a new element.

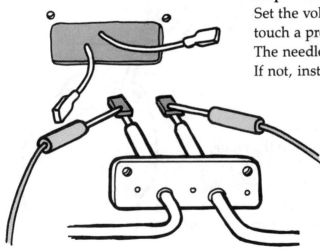

Step 7-10.
Testing the oven element for a short.
If the element shows continuity, touch one probe to one of the terminals and the other probe to the metal cover of the element. The needle should not move, indicating no connection. If it does move, replace the element with a new one.
Install the new element in the reverse order, making sure all brackets are securely mounted.

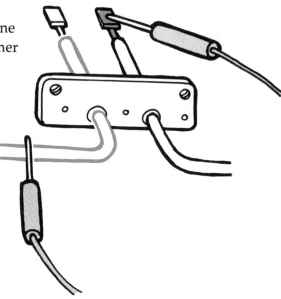

BACK PANEL

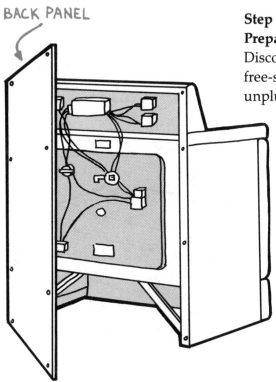

Step 7-11.
Preparing to check the burner switches.
Disconnect the power to the range. If it is a free-standing range, pull it away from the wall, unplug it, and remove the back panel.

Step 7-12.
Removing the control panel.
If the controls are mounted on the front of the range, remove the screws holding the control panel in place.

Step 7-13.
Removing the control panel's rear panel.
If you have a built-in range with the controls mounted on the backsplash, spread an old towel on top of the stove for protection. Then remove the screws from each end cap, tilt the backsplash forward, and remove the rear panel. You should now have access to the burner switches, the oven temperature control, and the oven selector switch. You should also notice the wiring diagram.

Step 7-14. Testing the burner switches.

Inspect each burner switch for visible damage, such as burned wire connections or loose connectors. Replace any damaged switch. The wires supplying power to the switch are connected to terminals marked L1 and L2. Wires running to the burner element might be numbered 1 and 2 or marked H1 and H2 (see the wiring diagram). Disconnect the wires marked L1 and L2 from the suspect switch. Set the volt-ohmmeter to the $R \times 1$ scale. Touch one probe to the terminal marked L1 and the other probe to each of the terminals connected to the wires leading to the burner element. You do not have to disconnect the element wires. As long as you have the other side of the switch (L1 and L2) disconnected, you can test the switch. With the switch on, the needle should move, indicating continuity. With the switch off, the needle should not move, indicating no connection. Repeat the test with one of the probes touching the terminal marked L2 and the other probe touching each of the element wire terminals in turn. Repeat the test on a burner switch that you know works properly, and compare the results. If the readings don't match, replace the suspect switch with a new one.

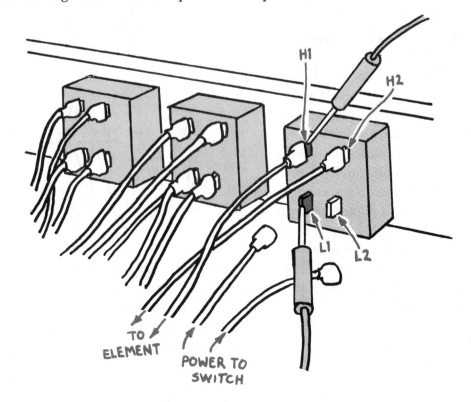

Step 7-15.

Installing a new switch.

When installing the new switch, label the wires and draw a simple wiring diagram before disconnecting the wires, or leave the wires connected to the old switch and transfer them one at a time to the new switch.

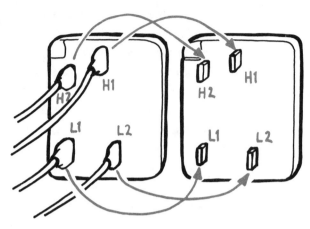

Step 7-16.

Checking the oven selector switch.

With the power disconnected and the control panel removed, look at the wiring diagram and locate the terminals for each setting (bake, broil, time bake, etc.) on the selector switch. You should see a pair of terminals for each setting. Disconnect one wire from each pair of terminals. Use a continuity tester or a volt-ohmmeter set to the R×1 scale and touch one probe to each of the terminals in the pair. The needle on the meter should swing to 0, showing continuity. Check each setting on the switch. If any setting fails the test, install a new switch. To install a new switch, label each wire and draw a simple wiring diagram. Disconnect the wires and remove the old switch from its mounting. Mount the new switch and reconnect the wires to the proper terminals.

Step 7-17. Testing the oven temperature control.

With the power turned off and control panel removed, use
a continuity tester or a volt-ohmmeter set on the R×1 scale
to check the oven temperature control for continuity. If more
than two wires are connected to the control, refer to the
wiring diagram on the inside of the control panel or on the
back panel to determine which pair of terminals to test. Now
disconnect one wire from the pair of terminals you are testing,
turn the control switch to about 300 degrees F, and touch a
probe to each of the two terminals. If the needle fails to move,
indicating no continuity, install a new temperature control.

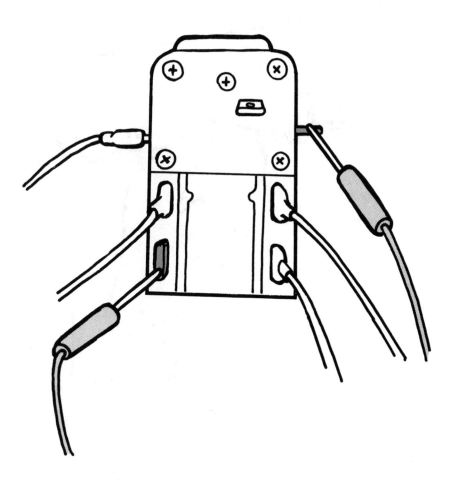

Step 7-18. Installing a new oven temperature control.
To replace the oven temperature control, first carefully unclip
the capillary tube from its supports in the oven and gently
push it through the rear wall. *Caution*: If this oven is a self-cleaning
model, wear rubber gloves and goggles—the tube is probably filled
with highly corrosive chemicals. If you happen to get any of these
chemicals on your skin, put the entire area under a steady flow of
running water immediately. Then seek medical help. With the wires
all labeled and disconnected, disconnect and remove the temperature
control and the capillary tube. Install a new temperature control and
connect the wires to the proper terminals. Next install the new
capillary tube, being careful not to bend or break it.

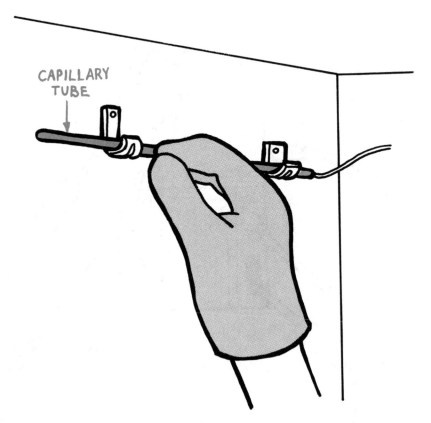

CAPILLARY
TUBE

Step 7-19.
Checking the calibration of the oven temperature control.
Place an oven thermometer on a rack in the middle of the oven.
Turn the oven on and adjust the temperature to 350 degrees F.
Heat the oven about 20 minutes. Then check the thermometer.
Write down the temperature. Check the thermometer 3 more times
at 10-minute intervals, recording the temperature at each check.
The average of these readings should be within 25 degrees of the
350-degree setting to be normal. If your average is off by 50 degrees,
recalibrate the temperature control. If the average is off by more
than 50 degrees, replace the temperature control with a new one.

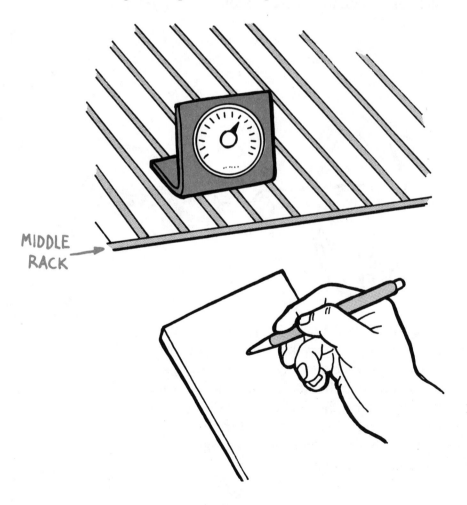

MIDDLE
RACK

Step 7-20. Calibrating the oven temperature control.
To calibrate the oven temperature control on some ovens,
pull off the control knob and look on its back side.
Loosen any screws or clips and turn the movable disk
in the direction marked on the knob to raise or lower
the temperature. You first might have to loosen a
retaining screw that holds the disk in its set
position. Typically, one notch represents a
10-degree change in temperature. If moving the
disk more than two notches is required to adjust the
thermostat, install a new temperature control (Step 7-18).

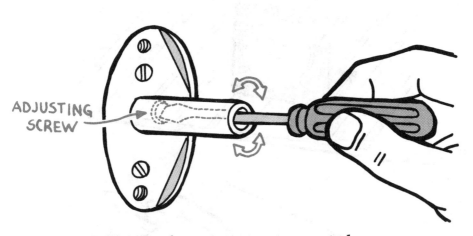

ADJUSTING
SCREW

Step 7-21. Calibrating the oven temperature control.
To calibrate the oven temperature control on other ovens,
pull off the control knob and locate the adjusting screw
inside the hollow shaft that fits into the knob. Turning the
screw clockwise lowers the temperature setting; turning
the screw counterclockwise raises it. Turn the screw very
slightly. If it requires more than about an eighth of a turn,
install a new temperature control (Step 7-18).

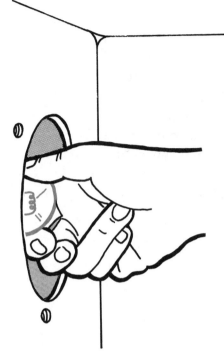

Step 7-22. Replacing the oven bulb.

Turn off the power to the range and remove the glass shield covering the bulb. Using gloves or a dry cloth, unscrew the bulb. Screw a 40-watt bulb into the socket. Restore the power. If the bulb lights, the old bulb was faulty. Remove the 40-watt bulb and install an appliance bulb of the proper size and wattage. Reinstall the shield. If the light bulb wasn't the problem, check the light switch.

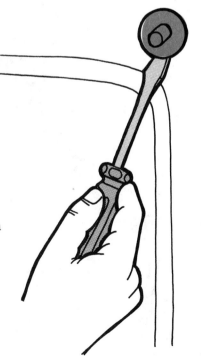

Step 7-23. Removing the light switch.

Turn off the power and open the oven door. Use a screwdriver to carefully pry the switch from the front of the oven.

Step 7-24. Testing the light switch.
Disconnect the wires from the switch's terminals. Use a continuity tester or volt-ohmmeter set on the R×1 scale to test the switch for continuity. Touch a probe to each of the two terminals on the switch. The needle should move, showing continuity. Now push in the switch plunger. The needle should swing in the other direction, showing no continuity. If your results differ, install a new switch. Connect the wires to the new switch and press the switch back into the opening.

PLUNGER

Glossary

capacitor A device used to store a charge of electricity.

circuit breaker
A safety switch installed in a circuit
that automatically interrupts the flow
of electricity if the current exceeds a
predetermined amount. Once tripped,
a circuit breaker can be reset manually.

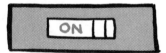

compressor
A machine that compresses,
or reduces the volume of, air or gas.

condenser
A device used to convert
gases or vapors to a liquid.

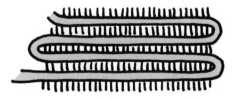

continuity   The state of having a continuous electrical path.

evaporator
A device used to change
a liquid into vapor.

idler pulley
A pulley used to take the
slack out of a drive belt.

insulator
A nonconducting material.

ohm   The unit for measuring electrical resistance.

relay
A switch operated
by an electromagnet.

resistance   That which opposes the flow of an
electrical current; measured in units called ohms.

service entrance panel
The main power cabinet containing the main breaker and circuit breakers distributing electricity throughout the residence.

solenoid
A coil of wire that uses an electrical current to create a magnetic field.

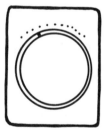

terminal
A point used to make electrical connections.

thermostat
A device used to control temperatures to a predetermined level.

volt-ohmmeter
A meter used for measuring voltage and electrical resistance.

Index

A

adjustable wrench, 2, 39, 59, 87

B

bulb, oven, 121
burner switches, preparing to check, 113
burners, 109

C

clothes dryer, 39-58
clothes washer (*see also* washer), 19-38
compressor relay, 74-75
compressor, refrigerator, 77
condenser coils, refrigerator, 62
condenser fan, 72-74
continuity tester, 39, 59, 79, 88, 107
control panel
    dishwasher, 89-93
    dryer, 42-46
    range, 114
    washer, 22-26
cycle selector switch, dishwasher, 92-93

D

defrost timer, 70-72
detergent dispenser, dishwasher, 94
dishwasher, 86-104
    control panel, 89-93
        control access, 90
        removal, 90
        unscrewing, 89
    cycle selector switch, 92-93
        checking, 92
        replacing, 93
    detergent dispenser, 94
    door gasket, 104
    door panel, removal, 89
    door switch,
        checking, 93-94
        installation, 94
    drain valve, 99
    drain valve solenoid, 99-100
        replacement, 100
        testing, 99
    float switch, testing, 98
    float, checking, 98
    heating element, 100-102
        checking, 100
        installation, 102
        removal, 101
    short, testing for, 101
    lower front panel, removal, 95
    parts, 87, 95
    spray arm, 102-103
        checking, 102
        cleaning, 103
        removal, 103
    telescoping spray tower, 102
    timer motor, testing, 91
    timer,
        replacement, 92
        testing, 91
    tools and materials, 88
    water inlet valve, 96-97
        removing and replacing, 97
door gasket, dishwasher, 104
door panel, dishwasher, 89
door switch, 47-48, 64, 93-94
    dishwasher, 93-94
    dryer, 47-48
    refrigerator, 64
drain valve solenoid, dishwasher, 99-100
drain valve, dishwasher, 99
drive belt, washer, 35
drum, dryer, 53-54

dryer, clothes, 39-58
control panel, removal,
42
controls, 42-46
gaining access, 42
start switch, testing, 46
temperature selector,
testing, 45
timer, 43-44
testing motor, 44
testing of, 43-44
door switch, 47-48
gaining access,
type one, 47
type two, 47
testing, 48
drum, 53-54
drive belt,
installation, 58
removal, 53
replacing, 57-58
removal, 54
removal, preparing for,
53
retaining clip, removal,
54
heater box, removal, 51
heating coils, 55-56
installing, 56
removal of, 55
testing, 52
heating element, 50-51
replacement, 51
testing, 50
parts, 40
thermostat, testing, 48-49
tools and materials, 39

E

electric ranges, 105-122
electric water heaters, 1-18
element, oven, 111-113
emery board, 107
energy-saver switch, 67
evaporator cover,
refrigerator, 68
evaporator fan, 69-70

G

gasket
door, dishwasher, 104
refrigerator door, 63
water heater, 15
gears, ice maker, 81
gloves, 4, 107
goggles, 107

H

heaters, electric water, 1-18
heating coils, dryer, 55-56
heating element, 14-15,
50-51, 100-102
dishwasher, 100-102
dryer, 50-51
water heater, 14-15
high-temperature cutoff,
7-8
replacement, 8
water heater, 7

I

ice maker, 78-86
cover removal, 80
gears, looking for, 81
internal parts, 81
motor, 83
mounting plate, removal,
81
on/off switch, 82
holding, 82
testing, 82
parts, 78
removal, 80
thermostat, 83-84
removal, 83
testing, 84
tools and materials, 79
water inlet valve switch,
testing, 82
water inlet valve,
disconnecting, 85
testing, 85

K

knife, kitchen, 79

L

lid safety switch, washer,
28-29
light bulb
40-watt, 107
oven, 121

M

motor, washer, 36-38
mounting plate, ice maker,
81

O

oven element, 111-113
removing, 112
short, testing for, 113
testing, 112
overload protector,
refrigerator, 76

P

pressure relief valve,
installation, 18
pipe wrench, 3
pliers, 21, 88
needle-nose, 21, 39, 107
pressure dome, 27
pressure relief valve, 17-18
old, 17
removal, 18
pump, washer, 33-34
putty knife, 39, 59

R

range, 105-122
burner, element, 108-109
checking, 109
receptacle, checking,
110
receptacle, replacing,
111

short, testing for, 110
terminals, testing of,
109
top, 108
switches, burner
preparing to check,
113
testing, 115
control panel,
rear panel, removing,
114
removing, 114
oven bulb, replacing, 121
oven control, calibration,
120
oven element,
removing, 112
short, testing for, 113
testing, 112
parts, 106
switch, light, 121-122
removal of, 121
testing of, 122
switches,
burner, testing of, 115
installing new, 116
oven, checking, 116
oven, temperature
control, testing of, 117
temperature control,
117-120
calibration, 119
installation, 118
tools and materials, 107
top element, checking,
108
ranges, 105-122
electric, 105-122
refrigerators, 59-77
compressor relay, 74-75
checking, 74-75
testing, 75
short testing, 77
compressor, testing, 77
condenser coils, cleaning
of, 62
condenser fan, 72-74

motor, 73-74
replacement, 74
short, 73
testing, 73
testing, 72
defrost timer, 70-72
location, 70
replacement, 72
test one, 71
test two, 71
door gasket,
replacement, 63
door switch, 64-65
removal, 64
testing, 65
energy-saver switch, 67
evaporator cover,
removal, 68
evaporator fan, 69-70
motor replacement, 70
removal, 68
testing motor, 69
insulation, removal, 68
light, checking, 64
overload protector, 76
testing, 76
removal, 76
parts, 60
temperature control,
65-67
removal, 66
replacement, 67
testing, 66
tools and materials, 59
relief valve, 2
reset button, water heater,
6

S

screwdriver, 3, 39, 59, 79,
88, 107
shallow pan or towel, 88
socket wrench, 21
sockets, 21, 59, 79
spray arm, dishwasher,
102-103

steel wool, 107
strainers, 30

T

telescoping spray tower,
102
temperature control, 65-67,
117-120
calibration, 119
installation, 118
oven, 117-120
refrigerator, 65-67
thermometer, 59, 79
oven, 107
thermostat, 2, 9-12, 48-49,
83-84
bottom, 10
bottom, setting, 10
dryer, 48-49
ice maker, 83-84
installation, 12
removal, 11
top, 9
top, voltage testing, 9
timer motor, dishwasher, 91
timer
dishwasher, 91
washer, 23-24
tools
40-watt bulb, 107
continuity tester, 39, 59,
79, 88, 107
emery board, 107
gloves, 4, 107
goggles, 107
kitchen knife, 79
pipe tape, 3
pliers, 21, 88
needle-nose, 21, 39,
107
putty knife, 39, 59
screwdriver, 3, 21, 39, 59,
79, 88, 107
shallow pan or towel, 88
sockets, 21, 59
steel wool, 107

tools (*cont.*)
thermometer, 59, 79
oven, 107
toothbrush, 88
towel, 39
vacuum cleaner, 59
volt-ohmmeter, 3, 21, 39,
59, 79, 88, 107
wire cutter, 39
wire, stiff, 88
wrench,
adjustable, 2, 39, 59, 87
pipe, 2
small socket, 59, 79
socket, 16, 21
toothbrush, 88
towel, 39

V

vacuum cleaner, 59
volt-ohmmeter, 3, 21, 39,
59, 79, 88, 107

W

washer, 19-38
control panel, 22-26
removal, 22
controls, access to, 22
drive belt, tightening, 35
lid safety switch, 28-29
checking, 28
testing, 29
motor, 36-38

continuity, testing for, 37
installation, 38
parts, 36
removal, 37
short, testing for, 36
parts of, 20
pressure dome, 27
pump, 33-34
access to, 33
hoses, disconnecting, 34
removal of, 34
replacement,
preparation, 33
replacement, 33-34
timer motor, testing, 24
timer replacement, 23
timer testing, 23
tools and materials, 21
water inlet valve, 30
strainers, 30
type one, 30-31
type two, 32
water level switch, 25-26
air hose, 25
installation, 26
water temperature
switch, testing, 24
water heater, 1-18
draining, 15
element, installation, 16
gasket removal, 15
getting started, 4
heating elements, 14-15
checking, 14-15

short, 14
high-temperature cutoff, 7
replacement, 8
illustration, 2
power, checking for, 4-5
pressure relief valve,
17-18
installation, 18
old, 17
removal, 18
relief valve, 2
reset button, checking, 6
thermostat, 2, 9-12
bottom, 10
setting, 10
installation, 12
removal, 11
top, 9
voltage testing, 9
tools and materials, 3
water inlet valve switch
ice maker, 82
water inlet valve
dishwasher, 96-97
ice maker, 85
washer, 30-32
water level switch, 25-26
wire cutter, 39
wire, stiff, 88
wrench
adjustable, 2, 39, 59, 87
pipe, 2
small socket, 59, 79
socket, 16, 21